young adult MINISTRY in the 21st century

the encyclopedia of practical ideas

Bible studies
media and culture
outreach

spiritual growth

Loveland, Colorado
www.group.com

Group resources actually work!

This Group resource helps you focus on **"The 1 Thing®"**—a life-changing relationship with Jesus Christ. "The 1 Thing" incorporates our **R.E.A.L.** approach to ministry. It reinforces a growing friendship with Jesus, encourages long-term learning, and results in life transformation, because it's:

Relational
Learner-to-learner interaction enhances learning and builds Christian friendships.

Experiential
What learners experience through discussion and action sticks with them up to 9 times longer than what they simply hear or read.

Applicable
The aim of Christian education is to equip learners to be both hearers and doers of God's Word.

Learner-based
Learners understand and retain more when the learning process takes into consideration how they learn best.

Young Adult Ministry in the 21st Century: The Encyclopedia of Practical Ideas

Visit our Web site: **www.group.com**

Credits
Editors: Brad Lewis, Beth Robinson, and Carl Simmons
Creative Development Editor: Matt Lockhart
Chief Creative Officer: Joani Schultz
Copy Editor: Lyndsay E. Gerwing
Art Director/Book Designer: Helen H. Harrison, YaYe Design
Assistant Art Director: Jean Bruns
Cover Art Director/Designer: Jeff A. Storm
Illustrator: Nick Deakin
Production Manager: Peggy Naylor

Library of Congress Cataloging-in-Publication Data

Young adult ministry in the 21st century : the encyclopedia of practical ideas.-- 1st American pbk. ed.
p. cm.
ISBN 0-7644-2801-2 (pbk. : alk. paper)
1. Church work with young adults--Handbooks, manuals, etc. I. Group Publishing.
BV4447.Y52 2005
259'.2303--dc22

2005025479

10 9 8 7 6 5 4 3 2 15 14 13 12 11 10 09 08 07 06
Printed in the United States of America.

Table of Contents

Contributors

Thanks to the following men and women—pastors, writers, and leaders of young adult ministries—for providing the dozens of ideas in this volume.

David E. Embree

Kate S. Holburn

James W. Miller

Benjamin J. Nugent

Melissa S. Nugent

Julie L. Roller

Christina Schofield

Allison Tarka

Jason Tarka

Kelli B. Trujillo

Special thanks to Brad Lewis, the compiling editor, for his work in pulling all the ideas in this book together into one resource that will serve young adult ministry for years to come.

Introduction

Welcome to *Young Adult Ministry in the 21st Century: The Encyclopedia of Practical Ideas!*

Just what are you? A single adult, a college student, someone embarking on a career, a 20-something? While young adults can feel lost in some churches, we believe that God passionately loves them and has an unbelievable purpose in mind for them. Young adults are energetic, passionate, compassionate, and resourceful people. And when they give themselves completely to God's service, watch out—something amazing will happen!

The ideas in this book will help you guide young adults to love God with their whole hearts, to love others with a strong and pure love, and to zealously serve the church and the world around them with an enthusiastic and self-sacrificing spirit.

Within these pages, you'll find dozens and dozens of practical ideas that you can use with young adults. Best of all, you can use them today! These ideas are creative, practical, and hands-on. Whether you want to put together an activity to deepen your group's relationships, discuss the Christian themes in a secular movie, or dive in to a service project for the disadvantaged in your community, this book can help.

Because this book is a collection of practical ideas, we've worked hard to put it together in a practical way. Of course, you can read it cover to cover if you want. But it's designed as a reference tool. You might want to start in the Table of Contents, find an area of young adult ministry, and scan the tips and ideas from there.

Each section includes a list of leader tips to help you in that area of your ministry, a "Quick Study" Bible study and activity that will help young adults understand the value of that area of ministry, and, of course, all kinds of practical ideas you can use today.

When using these pages, you may want to specifically put copies of them in the hands of your group members. Therefore, please note that several pages throughout this book have been noted as "OK to copy." (Look for the logo shown in the margin.) If there are other pages with ideas you would like to copy for use with your immediate small group, you may do so. However, if the leader of another group or class wants copies of those ideas, then that leader must purchase a copy of this book.

We pray that the young adults you serve will reap eternal benefits from the ideas in this book. May God bless and use you and your ministry.

Section One: Relationships

If young adults are universally interested in anything, it's building relationships. Sure, they might want different levels of friendship, but you can almost guarantee that in today's culture, young adults long for connections with others.

Think about the stage of life at which young adults find themselves. Whether they're college age, just starting a career, or getting settled in life as 20-somethings, chances are they've moved several times in the past few years. The more frequent the moves, the easier it is to give up hope of finding satisfying and authentic relationships.

The good news is that the church is built on relationships and community. And our relationship with Jesus is the most authentic relationship we will *ever* have. In John 15:13, 15 Jesus told his disciples, "Greater love has no one than this, that he lay down his life for his friends," and then reminded them, "I have called *you* friends." The Bible says many times that we're all connected. We're family. In fact, Scripture says as Christians, we belong to one another. Think of what your young adult ministry group would be like if people felt truly loved and cared for the moment they entered the door.

By focusing on building real relationships in insightful, meaningful, and creative ways, your group can offer a remedy to young adults who are suffering from loneliness and isolation. Together with the other members of your group, you can help build deep and lasting ties within your group. You can help them discover a sense of belonging. You can create an environment in which young adults learn to bear one another's burdens and love one another with Christ's love.

Now that they're on their own, away from the friends they grew up with, some in your group might not even know how to make friends. They've never had to do it before; relationships just kind of happened when they were growing up. That's why the activities in this section are so important: They give young adults in your group opportunities and tools for connections they might not know how to create on their own. You can read through these activities in order (although they're not listed in any particular order), or you can scan for ideas that interest you and fit your group best.

In addition to the ideas and activities here, a great resource for creating relationships throughout your church or within your young adult group is Group's *Friendship First: The 1 Thing You Can't Live Without* (www.friendshipfirst.com). This 13-week program—which can be purchased as a churchwide package or in separate kits for church leaders, adults, youth, and children—takes a fun approach to learning (there is a *lot* of food involved) while bringing members of your church or group into deeper relationships with Jesus and with one another.

Whatever you decide, be open to the leading of the Holy Spirit. You might use the activities just as they are or use them to spark your own ideas. Have fun, get to know each other better, and start building those brotherly and sisterly bonds that will help you relate to each other in very real and significant ways.

Quick Study

Authentic Communication

Read Luke 9:43b-45 and the "to know" information in the following paragraph. Then, as a group, talk through the "to discuss" questions. Finally, help everyone remember the quick study by doing the activity in the "to do" section.

To know:

After Peter confesses that Jesus is the Messiah (Luke 9:18-21), he and some of the other disciples witness two extraordinary displays of power that seem to confirm this confession of faith: Jesus' transfiguration (Luke 9:28-36) and the casting out of a demon from a boy (Luke 9:37-43a). After Peter's confession, Jesus reminds the disciples (Luke 9:21-22) that he will be delivered into the hands of mere mortals. The disciples don't understand what Jesus is saying, and they're afraid to ask.

To discuss:

- Why are the disciples afraid to ask Jesus what he meant? Are they afraid of appearing ignorant? Do they prefer not to understand? Is there some other explanation?
- During New Testament times, many Jews expected the Messiah to defeat the Romans and re-establish David's kingdom. With that in mind, why might the disciples not want to understand Jesus?
- Read Luke 9:23-26, and answer the previous question again.
- How do we sometimes act like the disciples and avoid honest communication with others?
- How can we improve communication when people don't want to understand us? when we're afraid to understand?

To do:

Instruct the group to break into pairs and interview each other about the role communication has played in their relationships. They can ask questions such as

- What's the hardest part of communicating with others?
- How has the way you communicate with friends changed over the years you've known them?
- What important communication or relationship tip do you wish everyone knew?

5 Leader Tips on Relationships

TIP 1

7 Ways of Welcome!

As leader, part of your job is to do whatever it takes to make young adults feel welcome in your group, as well as make sure they have opportunities to form deep and lasting friendships. Here are some ideas:

1. *Form a welcoming committee.* Find friendly people to greet everyone arriving at the group's activities, to explain what the agenda is for the day, and to chat with people before the day's events get started.

2. *Provide clear, complete information about your young adult ministry programs.* It's easy to come up with catchy titles for different events but then neglect to explain what those activities are for, when they meet, where they meet, and how long meetings last.

3. *Form a friend-making team.* Recruit a team of friendly group members to purposefully look for other young adults both at your ministry events and at larger church meetings. The friend-making team serves two purposes: It helps get young adults connected in real friendships, and it encourages young adults to move outside their regular group of friends.

4. *Don't expect too much right away.* You can easily fall into the trap of asking new people to bare their souls or sign away their lives to the young adult ministry, but that can scare them away. Instead, be friendly, warm, and accepting. Offer sincere friendship. Offer as much information as you can about your programs. But also respect people's privacy by allowing them to ease into your ministry as they feel comfortable.

5. *Provide multiple entry points for service.* The young adults in your ministry who will feel most connected to others will be the ones who volunteer to help lead.

6. *Watch out for cliques.* This isn't just a problem with junior high kids. If you notice that the same people always sit together and that others always sit

alone, come up with a plan to shake up the seating and help group members interact with new people.

7. Don't just watch the numbers. It's easy to assume that well-attended events are successful. But it may be that some people will come to event after event without ever truly connecting with another human being. Aim to provide some discussion time at every event, and encourage young adults to chat in pairs or trios to help them get to know one another. Also be sure to have a balance of large-group and small-group opportunities. Always try to help young adults deepen their connections to the group by getting them involved with a smaller set of group members who meet regularly.

TIP 2

Faces Old and New

It can be hard to keep up with new faces in your group. Make a copy of the chart on page 17 and, if possible, keep it with you at all times. List names of young adults you'd like to contact and why. Then, when you have a few spare moments, you'll be ready to give someone a quick call or send an e-mail.

If your ministry has a leadership team or volunteers for special events, you can also use this form to touch base with them and see how things are going in the areas they're responsible for. Be sure to pray for the people you contact as soon as you've finished talking to them.

TIP 3

Create a Young Adult Directory

Help young adults get to know one another with a directory.

Photocopy the form on page 18, enlarging it by about 15 percent to create an 8½x11 sheet. Ask each person in your young adult ministry to fill out a copy as completely as possible. Then gather all the forms, make copies, and put them in inexpensive, plastic three-ring binders.

Always have blank forms available at your young adult ministry events so new people can fill out forms and be included in the directory. Also be sure to always have copies of the directory available to hand out to young adults who are new to your group. Don't forget to photocopy forms turned in by new group members so current members can update their directories.

Touching Base

Name	Phone number/ e-mail address	Date Contacted	Comments	Prayer

Young Adult Ministry Directory

Name:

Address:

Phone number:

E-mail address:

Birthday:

Family or roommates (include names, ages, relationships, and birthdays when appropriate):

During the week, I fill my days by:

My favorite things to do for fun are:

I'm really good at:

I'd like to serve by:

My favorite foods are:

I started coming to this church in [year]:

I became active in the young adult group in [year]:

My favorite thing about this group/church is:

My favorite Scripture verses are:

What I would like the rest of the group to know about me is:

TIP 4

5 Quick Relationship Questions

Use these basic questions to build connections and friendships among the members of your group.

1. Who's your best friend, and why are you such good friends?
2. Do you like having a lot of friends or a few very close friends?
3. What qualities do you look for in a friend?
4. What do you need to change about yourself in order to be a better friend?
5. What's the best thing your friends would say about having you as their friend?

TIP 5

5 Easy Ways to Encourage Young Adults

Young adults are at a stage of life at which they face nearly constant change, turmoil, and indecision. Yet it often takes just a simple word of encouragement to lift someone's day or week. Try these suggestions for urging young adults in your group to "hang in there."

1. *Follow up on prayer requests.* Many times a prayer request is for an event on a specific date. Job interviews, medical tests, and even awkward family gatherings are examples of things group members may request prayer for. Make a phone call that day to say you were praying and to find out how things went.

2. *Make a phone call before an event.* This is similar to the previous idea, except that you call *before* the difficult experience. Make a brief phone call the evening before, and let the member of your group know that you'll be praying for him or her. You can even offer to pray on the phone together.

3. *Buddy chores.* Give a member of your young adult group your assistance for a morning. Ask when you can come over and help with a task. Most jobs go better when two work together. Even better, gather the whole group to tackle a job for one. A group of people can accomplish a lot of yardwork or help someone move to a new home in a short time.

4. *Encouragement out of nowhere.* Send a young adult group member a note to encourage him or her to keep on being faithful. Include a few personalized

Scripture verses. Ask the Lord to help you sense when someone may need a gentle embrace.

5. Send an article or cartoon. If you see a humorous or inspirational item that relates to something going on in a group member's life, send it. A sticky note saying, "I saw this and thought of you" is all that's necessary.

25 Relationship-Building Ideas

IDEA 1
Let's Talk

Why not start your efforts to deepen relationships among the young adults in your group with a special event night focusing on, of all things, relationships.

In advance, invite a panel of people from your group (or other leaders from your church) to sit at a table in front of the group. This panel can lead a forum-type exploration of all facets of relationships: communication, fun, acceptance, love, boundaries, selflessness, fellowship, faith, and so on. Encourage participation by dividing the group into pairs or trios to come up with questions for the panel.

You can also choose panel members who represent different types of relationships—best friends, family connections, married couples, or dating relationships. The questions group members ask the "experts" will spark an authentic discussion on the joys and struggles of relationships.

Throughout the evening, focus on biblical truths and God's desire for young adults to have deep and healthy relationships that center on Jesus. Explore Scripture verses such as Psalm 145:8-10, 13-21 and Romans 5:6-11 for the qualities Jesus displayed as a friend and how it's possible for Christians to emulate those characteristics.

After the panel presentation, divide your group into smaller groups of four or five to discuss what they've discovered. These questions might help focus the small-group discussions:

- What are the most important qualities to have in any relationship, and why?
- What are the differences between certain types of relationships—best friends, marriage, family, and so on?
- What parts of your relationships are the easiest for you? the hardest?

IDEA 2

Making Space

The members of your young adult group are probably pretty similar when it comes to age, cultural identification, marital status, parental status, and economic status. This simple exercise will help group members be more open to the possibility that their experiences will be richer when they're learning from a more diverse group of people.

Take an informal survey of your group by discussing group members' ages, cultural backgrounds, racial backgrounds, and so forth. Or simply ask the group how they would generally classify themselves.

Then schedule a meeting of your group in a place where the population is different from most of your group members. For example, travel to another side of your city or to a nearby town with a strong ethnic influence or a dominant age demographic obviously different from your group's. During your meeting, discuss the following:

- How does meeting here make you feel? Why?
- Describe what it feels like to be surrounded by people who are different from you.
- Why do you think it can be uncomfortable to be around people who aren't like you?
- Read Galatians 2:6-16; 3:26-28; and Revelation 7:9-10. How can our church become a community where people embrace others who are unlike them?
- How can a community with a variety of people be beneficial?
- What can you do to make space for others and embrace differences?
- If we wanted to embrace the people from the area we're in now, what could we do?

IDEA 3

Friendship Field Trip

One way young adults can explore how God strengthens relationships is by traveling as a group to locations representing those different kinds of relationships. Think of places where young adults—including those beyond your group—spend time investing in their relationships, as well as places that simply symbolize certain kinds of relationships. Some ideas for locations include

- coffee shops or restaurants
- college campuses

- neighborhood streets or city blocks
- church buildings
- gyms or fitness clubs
- places of business
- movie theaters
- clubs or bars (exercise wisdom on this one)

At each location, form groups of three or four, and find non-distracting, out-of-the-way spots for these smaller groups to gather. Have each group read 1 Samuel 16:7; Matthew 5:14-16; Colossians 3:12-13; and James 1:19-20. Encourage groups to spend time praying for God's touch of growth and healing for each group member's relationships.

After praying, have groups answer these questions:

- What are some unique things about each of your relationships?
- What kind of relationships do you think are represented by this place?
- What do you value most about the kinds of relationships that take place here?
- How can you actively, and regularly, dedicate your relationships to God?
- In what ways would you like to see God strengthen each of your relationships?

IDEA 4

Taking the Time to Listen

A skill that becomes increasingly more valuable in our society is the ability to listen. Especially as young adults begin taking on more responsibilities—work, school, family—the temptation to rush through their lives and relationships, whether with others or with Christ himself, becomes easier to give in to. Learning to listen actively (and it *is* a skill that can be learned) helps us overcome "the tyranny of the urgent" and keep our focus on what's really important.

In preparation for your next group meeting, write several conversation starters on slips of paper; make sure you have enough slips for everyone in the group. Some suggestions for conversation starters (to get *you* started) include "Someday I'd like to..." "A really cool place I'd like to go on vacation is..." "A news story that interested me recently was..." "Something I'm really passionate about is..." Put all your slips in a container.

When your group gathers, ask:

- What does it mean to be a good listener?
- Why is it important to be a good listener?

Ask your group to break off into pairs. Encourage group members to pair up with people they don't know. ask each group member to draw a conversation starter from the container. Instruct group members that one person will listen attentively while the other talks for up to three minutes on the subject listed on his or her slip. After three minutes, call time and have pairs reverse roles.

After three more minutes, call time and gather the group back together. Then ask:

- What did you learn about the person you were paired with?
- What was it like to be a good listener?
- What did you most appreciate about being listened to?

Together, read John 10:3-4, 14-16 and James 1:19, and then ask:

• How does listening help us serve others better? How does it help us, personally?

• In what ways is listening to a friend similar to how God listens to us? how we listen to God?

• What keeps us from listening to God? What helps us listen to God?

• What changes can we make to be better listeners with our friends? with God?

IDEA 5

T-Shirts for the Gang

Bands have uniforms, football teams wear matching jerseys, and even gangs sport "colors." Why? One reason is that the similar clothing promotes unity and togetherness.

Have your group members create T-shirts to give them an opportunity to work together and provide another connection point. Brainstorm about things that make your group unique. Maybe you've shared an experience that produced a "tagline" that everyone in your group enjoys, such as "It can't be more than a couple more miles," or "No problem—I've done this a hundred times."

If you have any artistic types in your group, they can probably come up with something ready to be silk-screened. But if your group is "artistically challenged," many screen-printing shops have artists who can clean up your artwork "draft." Poll your group regarding favorite colors, and get a list of sizes. Then get your shirts into production. Order extras for those who forget and for new members who come along.

Another idea is to have a simple logo screened onto inexpensive white

T-shirts and then hold a tie-dye party to make each shirt unique. You'll find simple instructions for tie-dyeing at www.kinderart.com/textiles/easytiedye.shtml.

When your shirts are finished, wear your colors! Introduce your team spirit to the rest of your church by encouraging all group members to wear the shirts to the same event. You can also wear them for service projects and group events, as well as at other social activities.

IDEA 6
Nighthawks

A lot of young adults, by nature, are nocturnal creatures, living much of their lives well after dark. Many of their best friendships and most meaningful conversations come out of late-night sessions of one kind or another.

Create a new tradition for your young adult group. Establish later-night hangout times weekly, monthly, or at an interval that fits the group best. These get-togethers seem to work best as "come with no agenda and let the conversations flow" gatherings.

What makes a late-night meeting different from others you'll have? A good location for getting together after dark has both a character of its own and good coffee. Guys tend to like "holes in the wall" with names like "Pappy's Barbecue: Home of the 24-Hour Breakfast Special," where the rest of the customers are truckers (or at least could be). Women might feel safer at franchise places like Starbucks that are well lit and predictable. Prayerfully consider what atmosphere and location works best for the particular members of your group and for those you're seeking to attract to your group.

Announce that you'll be getting together with anyone who wants to at 11 on a particular night, and you'll attract a wide sampling of people from your group. They'll show up with different motives and needs. Because of the unusual gathering time, they may wind up sitting with people they don't usually sit with and telling stories they don't usually tell—and they'll realize that they have more in common with other members of your group than they thought.

If people do sit with the same cluster of people week after week, have a mandatory "shuffle" time every half hour or so the first few times, and they'll figure out that this is a time for stretching relationships.

Hang out for two or three hours, and tip the wait staff well when you leave. You can check out a new place each month or make one cafe your regular hangout.

IDEA 7
My Pals

The difference between an acquaintance and a friend comes down to the amount of shared history two people have. "Members of my young adult group" become "my pals" as soon as they can start saying, "Remember when we..."

How do you make memories? You share experiences. While good and important things happen in Bible studies and worship times, seldom does something happen that really bonds people together in those settings. "Remember when we all sat in chairs and read out of the Bible?" Not the stuff that makes for touching reunions later in life!

Set a date for your group to go out and experience something together. If your group is large, split it into smaller groups of five to seven people each. What to do? Encourage your young adults to be creative—and they will be. A few suggestions:

- Have a picnic that begins with the group shopping for food together.
- Go to a nearby vacation spot, and have fun being "tourists."
- Milk the cows or shear the sheep at someone's home farm.
- Take a bike ride to a nearby lake.
- Take a road trip to a minor league ball game.
- Work on a Habitat for Humanity project together for a day.

You'll be amazed at what groups come up with. And you'll be amazed at what happens within the group. Those who participate will come back with stories and jokes and the beginnings of completely different relationships with one another.

Encourage groups to take a lot of photos. You might even provide disposable cameras for each group to use. Share the pictures with your larger group later to celebrate your new sense of family.

IDEA 8
Life Journey Map

This activity will build insight and vulnerability among members of a small group. You'll need:

- heavy-duty white construction paper (at least one sheet per person)
- colored lightweight paper
- glue and/or tape

• markers, pens, and pencils
• stickers
• scissors
• old magazines (ask group members to bring these so you have plenty of materials to choose from)

Individuals will use these materials to create maps describing their life stories. The maps can be linear, showing the chronological order of their major life events. Or the maps can be "circular," illustrating their life cycles of learning experiences. The maps can be as detailed as each individual feels comfortable. However, the more vulnerable people are, the deeper the group can grow as a whole. So encourage people to push the limits of their comfort zones a bit.

To get creative juices flowing, tell group members to think about people who've had a strong influence in their lives—both good and bad. Also, encourage them to think through times of stagnation, growth, confusion, and peace. Read Acts 26; 2 Corinthians 6:3-13; and Philippians 4:10-13. The Apostle Paul provides a great example of being vulnerable about his life experiences and lessons. In fact, group members could be encouraged to read all of 2 Corinthians before your meeting—this book is considered to be one of Paul's most personal letters.

When the maps are finished, ask each person to "show and tell." As each person shares, these questions might lead to deeper discussions:

• Which points along the way have been major learning points, and what did you learn?
• What cycles has your life taken?
• Where is God in your map?
• What role does God play in your life now? How has that role changed over the course of your life so far?
• What do you see as a potential next step in your life?

IDEA 9

Removing the Mask

This exercise will help young adults in your group recognize that the external impression they give people may not accurately reflect what's going on inside. You need paper and pens. Be sure your group is already a place where members feel safe and comfortable to share reflectively.

Read Isaiah 29:13, and say, "Authenticity is important to God. What we say and do should match what's really going on inside. This is so important that Jesus repeated these words in Matthew 15:8-9."

Now ask your group members to close their eyes, and have each of them imagine they're in a public place they go to on a regular basis—their jobs, the grocery store, church, wherever it might be. Ask them to focus on what others in that place observe about them externally. After a few minutes, ask them to write down what impression they're trying to make, or believe they're making, on their external world.

Then ask your group members to close their eyes again. This time, they should imagine arriving home or someplace that feels like home. Ask them to think about what someone would observe about them at "home." After a few minutes of thinking time, ask them to write down what their internal worlds look like. What do they think about, and how do they feel when they let down their guard? What is true about them in this "safe place" that others don't usually see?

Instruct your group to get together for discussion, and work through the following questions:

- Is there is a gap between your external and internal lives? If so, where is it, and why?
- Is this gap favorable to have in every situation?
- Is there a time a gap may be a good thing?
- How can you be more authentic in your external world?
- Why do you sometimes hesitate to be genuine?

After discussing these questions, have the members of your group imagine that they're back in the same public place where this exercise began. But this time, ask them to think about what it looks like to be there in a truly authentic way. Ask the following questions:

- What does it look like to be "real" in a public place?
- What steps do you need to take to make this a reality?

IDEA 10

Community in Nature

Head to a nearby park or wooded area for an inspirational group walk. Break the larger group into subgroups of two or three people each, and have the groups head off in various directions.

Each group's task is to find examples about community in God's creation. Remind the group that 1 Corinthians 12:12-31 provides a clear illustration of community by comparing it to the human body. Some parts are honorable and some less; some parts are for smelling and others for seeing.

Give the smaller groups about 30 minutes, and then have them reconvene to discuss the following:

- What illustration of community did your group find?
- What aspect of community does it show, and why?
- What did you see that made this a community?
- What can our communities, especially our church or our group, learn from the example you found in creation?
- What benefits come from being part of a thriving community?
- What happens when we lack this kind of community?
- What sacrifices do you need to make to be part of a healthy community?

IDEA 11
Making a Mosaic

Sometimes our lives are fragmented. Different parts of life coexist in tension because they're contrary to one another. It seems that most of us have an increasing lack of wholeness in our personal lives and in the ways we connect with others.

For this activity, you'll need:

- solid-colored tiles
- tile mastic
- old picture frames (check discount or secondhand stores)
- boards that fit the frames (consider cutting them from Lauan, a lightweight plywood available at most home-improvement stores)
- grout
- brushes and trowels
- hammers
- old cloths

Group members can help provide materials (or if your budget allows, most items can be purchased at a home-improvement store). You can save money by breaking up old ceramic dishes from a garage sale. And check the broken tile bin while you're at the home-improvement store.

Before you start, ask group members to consider areas such as family, friends, a significant other, career, hobbies, or other activities. Then discuss the following questions:

- What areas of life feel whole for you? (Use a solid, whole piece of tile as a symbol of that wholeness.)

• What parts of your life seem fragmented? What areas exist in tension with each other? (Place a whole piece of tile under a cloth, and break it with a hammer.)

• Read Galatians 2:11-21. Even Peter had to be corrected by Paul regarding fragmented parts of his life that weren't biblical. With that in mind, how does it feel to live in tension where parts of your life don't fit together?

• Is this tension positive or negative for you? Explain.

• What part of that passage best summarizes your own thoughts on this tension?

Now have group members take tiles, safely break them inside the old cloths, and make their own mosaics. First, cover a board with mastic. Then press the pieces of tile into the mastic, allow them to dry, and then brush the grout between the tiles. This should allow enough time for group members to digest the discussion and continue talking about wholeness and fragmentation in their lives.

IDEA 12
Pushing the Limits

Though there's often not a lot of reality in television "reality" shows, the popularity of *Survivor, Fear Factor,* and *The Amazing Race* likely makes young adults wonder, "Could I? Would I?" Though the artificial challenges of these shows sometimes seem silly and occasionally mean-spirited, young adults often wonder how they would deal with similar challenges.

Jesus offers a faith that is completely countercultural: "Whoever loses his life for me and for the gospel will save it" (Mark 8:35). The young adults in your group need challenges in order for them to realize that they can do things they didn't think they were capable of.

Unless you're fully certified in the following areas, *do not* attempt to create these experiences yourself. Find local resources that have the expertise (and insurance) you can rely on, and engage them to safely provide these experiences for your group.

For beginning challenges, try climbing at a local climbing wall, scrambling into a "wild" cave, skiing on an indoor slope with artificial snow, or target practice at a shooting range.

The next level of adventure might include bungee jumping, paintball, wilderness climbing, or rappelling. Again, the goal isn't to arbitrarily put people into dangerous situations but to help provide opportunities for them to be stretched. Processing after the experience is more important than the activities.

For the adrenaline junkies in the group, it may take something major to push them beyond their previous limits, but helping them experience something that gets their blood flowing faster is worth the effort. Try whitewater rafting, skydiving, or even hunting wild boar!

After your group has faced its challenge together, take a good amount of time to debrief. Ask group members the following questions:

- What were some of the feelings you had as you began your challenge?
- How did those feelings change as you began to complete your challenge?
- How can this experience apply to our everyday adventures in life?
- What adventure is God inviting you to take on in your life right now?
- How will today's experience help you face the challenges you see ahead of you?

Whatever level your group's experience is at, it will generate stories that will be told for years to come, binding people together as friends. And as individuals come to recognize that they can do all sorts of things they never believed they could, they'll be more open to the idea that they can do the things Jesus calls them to, including things they thought were impossible. In the process, your young adults will become a group of fellow adventurers.

IDEA 13

Picture This

Purchase a large scrapbook as well as other craft supplies as needed. Present the scrapbook to your group, and explain that it is the relationship scrapbook that will belong only to the young adult ministry. It will be dedicated to group members' various personal relationships, and the group will continue updating it together as an ongoing experience.

This relationship scrapbook is a safe place for people to explore their relationships and welcome God into those relationships. They can record thoughts, memories, prayers, and Bible verses (suggest such passages as John 15:12-15; Ephesians 4:15; Philippians 2:1-3; and 1 John 4:7-8, 11-12), and place photos on the pages. Use the scrapbook to focus on relationships within the young adult ministry. People can write affirming notes to each other and paste into the scrapbook mementos of times they've had together.

Once a month, flip through the scrapbook, and share with each other both the new things about the relationships represented and additional thoughts and memories that may not even be in the book. Pray together for family members, friends, and others represented in the book's pages, asking that God would make these relationships strong and honoring to him. While working on and paging through the scrapbook together, talk about these questions:

- What were your feelings when you created these pages?
- What do you feel when looking at others' pages?
- How can our relationships grow stronger and honor God more and more?
- What does this scrapbook reveal about the relationships in our young adult group?
- How can we better encourage and pray for each other's relationships?

IDEA 14
Celebrating Each Other

Help the young adults in your group enjoy each other and celebrate the past *and* present. Throw a themed party together, modeled after dances or parties from high school. Depending on the theme, encourage attendees to wear clothes from prom, homecoming, weddings, thrift stores, and so on.

Ask volunteers to form a party committee that will plan the details of the throwback night, including party food, cheesy music, over-the-top decorations, a picture taken for arrivals, and games.

This celebration night will cause people to laugh together, enjoy great fellowship and fun, and create treasured memories.

During or after the event, eat together in small groups and discuss:

- How do fun times, such as tonight, affect friendships?
- How can our group weave more fun and fellowship into our times together? What will that do to our relationships?
- Read Acts 2:46-48. What does this passage tell us about the importance of friendship and joy in our relationships with Christ and others?

IDEA 15

Dueling Affirmation

Divide your young adult group into two equal groups. Each group's assignment is to come up with a creative way to affirm the other group. This can be done with food, service, a skit or video, gifts, an experience, or any combination. The only guideline is that it must be a surprise. Plan a Saturday when the two groups can "reveal" their creative affirmations, or plan for them to present their surprises separately. Group members should also tell each other what they appreciate and like about each other and why they are grateful for the gift of each other's friendship (see Ephesians 4:29 and 1 Thessalonians 5:11-15). Later, discuss the following questions together:

- How did it make you feel to give and receive this affirmation?
- What role does affirmation play in relationships?
- How can we intentionally affirm and encourage each other?

IDEA 16

"You've Got Prayer"

E-mail can be an easy way for a group of friends to share prayer requests and praises with one other. Set up an e-mail "prayer team" for each small group within your ministry or for a group of eight to 10 people within your large group.

Encourage each individual to e-mail the entire group on a regular basis (for example, weekly, on Mondays), including prayer requests for the upcoming week and praises for what God has done and how he has answered previous prayers.

Then encourage members of the group to reply to the writer of the e-mail with an e-mailed prayer response for the request(s). This could be as short as a one-sentence prayer or as long as a paragraph or two. For example, when Nick e-mails the group with a request for his mom's upcoming surgery, Joe might reply with this e-mail: "God, please guide the doctor's hands during Sharon's surgery tomorrow. Give them wisdom to know what to do, and help her heal quickly."

This experience allows all group members the opportunity to encourage one another with their prayers, rather than just promising to pray at some vague point in the future. During difficult times, these prayers can be reread as a reminder of the concern group members share for one another.

IDEA 17

Feed on the Word

Sharing meals together as Christians is a tradition that's been around since the days of the early church. Acts 2:46 says, "They broke bread in their homes and ate together with glad and sincere hearts." This can be a way to build relationships between today's young adults as well. This idea works best if small groups of young adults already meet together regularly for Bible study or fellowship. But you can also adapt it for larger groups.

Each week, the group will eat dinner (or lunch) together before the Bible study begins. Group members bring different dishes that follow a theme: Italian, Mexican, Chinese, homemade pizza (everyone brings toppings), soup and salad, or other ideas. A volunteer (or team), designated as the "meal planner," chooses the themes and then assigns in advance different group members to bring the parts of the meal.

If your young adult ministry doesn't already have small groups, build "meal groups" from within your large group. These groups could be encouraged to meet and eat together weekly or at some other regular interval. More important than what you eat is watching relationships grow. The idea isn't to force conversations by having discussion questions or a specific topic to talk about; rather, it's a time for relationships to develop and expand naturally while talking about work, the weekend, and anything else going on in your lives.

IDEA 18

Two Are Better Than One

While many young adults desire an authentic relationship with Christ, some aren't sure where to begin. People in this stage of life can have a difficult time "plugging in" with an authentic community.

Of course, a growing relationship with Christ is key to the spiritual growth of Christians. Some young adults can be scared off by the word *discipleship*; however, discipleship simply means coming alongside another Christian and helping that person grow in an authentic relationship with Jesus.

Help the young adults in your ministry seek out the wisdom of an older Christian in your group or church. Age isn't as important as where a person is on his or her own spiritual journey. Recruit spiritually mature members of your group and your church to pair up with those in your group who are younger in the faith. As the young adult leader, you can also be a great model for this type of ministry as you seek out younger Christians to help.

Encourage young adults to put their fears aside. Often all it takes is a simple invitation for a cup of coffee or a meal to begin an authentic relationship centered on getting to know Jesus better. You can start by simply asking, "What has God been teaching you lately?" Then you can share what you have been learning from your own times in the Bible, sermons at church, Christian music you've been listening to, or anything else God has used to speak to you.

Once you spend a few times together talking about what you've been learning, you can choose something new to study together. *The Gospel for Real Life* by Jerry Bridges is a great book for Christians of any age and maturity. It deals with the question of how the Gospel message should affect our daily lives as Christians—and not just on the day we made a commitment to Jesus. A Bible study on what the Gospel *really* is would be a powerful follow-up to reading this book. Another fantastic book by Jerry Bridges is *The Pursuit of Holiness,* or the more contemporary version titled *The Chase.*

The book of James is a very practical, applicable book of the Bible for someone who doesn't really know what it means to read the Bible and apply it to daily life. There are countless topical studies you could do together straight from the Bible, depending on an individual's needs. The key is to figure out what you'd like to study, choose something that relates, and then do it together!

IDEA 19
More Than a Checklist

A critical component to growth in your group members' relationships with Jesus is accountability. This word may conjure up stereotypes of legalistic checklists to make sure people are doing everything "necessary" in the Christian life or groups of people telling each other their deepest sins. However, accountability groups aren't rooted in legalism or behavior management. They should be rooted in love and a genuine desire to help one another grow.

Accountability can be a catalyst for growth, especially when done in a loving, gracious, and biblical way. This in no way means that you *condone* one another's sin, but the way you help each other overcome sin can be a tremendous blessing.

According to Hebrews 10:24-25, God wants us to meet together and encourage one another in order to become more like Christ. Accountability can take place within established small-group Bible studies, or it can be offered as a separate option for your young adults. For almost every issue, single-gendered groups work best. It's difficult to open up about sin when the groups are mixed. If that's not possible, coed studies can break into separate groups of men and women for accountability purposes during the last 20-30 minutes of their time together.

Each person can simply bring up issues with which he or she is struggling. Individuals can also share ways others in the group can help or ask for suggestions about what to do in a given situation. Galatians 6:2 tells us, "Carry each other's burdens, and in this way you will fulfill the law of Christ." For example, if someone is struggling with an addiction to Internet pornography, the group can arrange phone partners that he can call for prayer, encouragement, and a way out of sin (1 Corinthians 10:13). Prayer is vital in accountability groups.

Finally, don't always make the accountability group or time an intense period of confessing and repenting. Have some fun once in a while, organizing an activity or adventure together. This might be as simple as a movie night or as complex as a weeklong canoe trip in the wilderness to bond and enjoy God's creation. Your young adults will be more likely to share their lives with friends they value and enjoy.

IDEA 20
Game Night

It's game night—a great way for people within your ministry to meet and get to know each other in a completely nonthreatening setting. Host the game night at your church or at a home with room for everyone.

Prior to the event, collect from group members as many different board games as possible (such as Cranium, Pictionary, Guesstures, Taboo, or Outburst). Set up each game at a different table in the room, with plenty of chairs for two teams to play the game around the table. Be sure to leave the game rules out in case the game is new to someone.

Divide the group into random teams of four to eight people. Assign numbers as they walk through the door (and have those numbers on the game tables), or just ask group members to sit at tables with people they don't know very well.

Once everyone arrives, let the games begin! Set a timer for 20 minutes, and when it goes off, the games stop and the teams move to different game tables to face new opposing teams. Perhaps the winning team rotates clockwise and the losing team rotates counterclockwise. You can also remix the teams halfway through the evening.

The idea isn't to finish playing each game but for people to spend time with others who they might not see on a regular basis. This also can be a nonthreatening atmosphere to welcome new people into your ministry (by encouraging group members to invite friends). An event like this can create new relationships between people who may end up being friends for a long time.

IDEA 21

Nintendo and Nails

While encouraging relationships across the board in your ministry is a fantastic idea, it can also be great to encourage relationships among your men and women separately. These activities can be the beginnings of lifelong friendships, as well as accountability groups and other spiritually focused interactions.

Plan men's and women's social nights. It is best to schedule both for the same evening so every member of your ministry has an opportunity to attend.

For the women, organize a spa night featuring facials, manicures, pedicures, makeovers, and foot massages. This could be a "self-service" night where all the materials are available and women use them on their own, or you could get volunteers to actually perform the services. Other ideas include "romantic movie" night, craft night (stamping, scrapbooking, card-making), sewing night, or game night. Conversation will be plentiful, as these activities lend themselves well to getting to know each other. If your group is small enough, some of them might want to turn this night into a slumber party!

For the men, organize a video game marathon. Set up different systems in different rooms. Most guys from the group can help supply TVs, game systems, extra controllers, and games. Other ideas for men's nights include card games, men's movie night, sports night (in a church gym or elsewhere), bowling, or paintball.

Of course, snacks are a "must-have" for both events!

IDEA 22

Movin' On Up...

People in the young adult phase of life seem to always be on the move. College students move in and out of their dorms or apartments each school year. As people graduate from college, get jobs, start making more money, and maybe even get married, they may move several different times. Young adults might change roommates, change apartments, or change houses. These continual moves can be a perfect time for the young adults in your ministry to be a community to one another.

Let your young adults know that you would like "moving teams" to be a part of the group's ministry to each other. Ask them to let you know about upcoming moves, either their own or someone else's in the ministry. This can also be an outreach opportunity to help people who aren't a regular part of your ministry as well.

What do you need to make this a success? Volunteers! Most moves in this stage of life can be completed in a morning if there are enough people helping. Young adults just haven't accumulated enough stuff yet to make the move longer! Find a system that works for your ministry: e-mail, word of mouth, sign-up sheets, or another idea. Let volunteers know the needs for each particular move, as well as the dates and times. At a minimum, find out the following:

- Does the person need help packing the week before?
- Is the mover renting a moving van or looking for volunteers with trucks and/or trailers?
- Will he or she be ready to load the van on Friday night, or does everything need to happen on Saturday morning?

If you can pull together enough volunteers, it should be possible to load the van, drive it to the new location (if it's a local move), and unload it before lunch. Decide beforehand if the person who is moving will buy pizza for everyone for lunch to say thank you (a great idea) or if everyone will chip in to pay for it. Either way, having lunch together is a nice reward and a time to relax and talk a bit after all that hard work.

IDEA 23

More Than Powder-Blue Leisure Suits

Young adults seem to be most comfortable in a relaxed atmosphere, but it can also be fun to have a more formal event occasionally. Put together a semi-formal dinner and/or dance. Valentine's Day and Christmas can be good times of the year to schedule an event, but you can make it work any time of the year. Sometimes it can be even more fun to have a formal event for no special reason!

Stress that the event doesn't require anyone to bring a date. The idea is to have a fun reason to get dressed up and spend an evening together.

Items to consider in the budget for this event are decorations, a DJ (whether for a dance or for background music), food, and maybe some door prizes. Once you've determined your cost, you can decide on a ticket price if your young adult ministry budget can't cover the costs.

Start promoting the event several months before it takes place. Get group members excited about attending—and inviting their friends! Encourage the women in your group to dress up in old prom or bridesmaid dresses, with the men in suits or tuxes. If no one has these, make the formal clothing a thrift-store challenge—and offer prizes to the best dressed, the tackiest dressed, and the person who got the best deal.

You can also make this event less expensive by using fewer decorations, recruiting a member of the group to put together music on mix CDs or an iPod, and serving dessert. On the other end of the spectrum, you could "do it up" big with lots of decorations, a DJ, and a full meal at a hotel banquet room.

Either way, as long as there are tables, chairs, and plenty of time to talk, the young adults in your group will enjoy spending this time together. It's a great change from the way they are used to relating to one another, and it's fun to see each other all dressed up!

IDEA 24
Softball, Soccer, and a Savior

Sports are an almost universal way to develop relationships between people. Form a team (or multiple teams) of group members to join a local sports league. Check for leagues through the local YMCA or your community's parks and recreation department. There might even be interchurch leagues for sports such as softball. Many sports offer coed leagues as well as all-men and all-women teams.

These leagues can be a great way for young adults to develop authentic relationships with one another, as well as with other players of other teams. A common interest in sports is a great platform for developing friendships.

If no league exists in your area, consider starting one! There may be young adults from other local churches interested in playing. Even just a few teams can work. Plus, this is an easy way to take relationships that begin within church walls and take the light of Christ into your community.

IDEA 25
Did Someone Say "Road Trip"?

Sometimes half the fun in going somewhere is enjoying the ride. Plan a young adult group day trip. The destination isn't as important as the idea that you're going somewhere together.

First, decide where you want to go. It could be as simple as driving to a town an hour or two away, grabbing a meal there, and heading home. Or it could be traveling for a bigger event like a concert or a play. If you're from a bigger city, it might be fun to travel to a smaller town and enjoy a slower-paced day. Or if you live in a small town, a trip to a bigger city is always an adventure.

Next, figure out who wants to go and who can drive. then arrange carpools so that new relationships can be fostered among people who don't know each other well.

Decide if you have money in your budget to provide gas for each car or if you'd like passengers to contribute gas money to the drivers. Also, be sure participants know the cost of the destination event. You can choose to keep the destination a secret until you leave, providing drivers with maps in the parking lot. Or you can let everyone know ahead of time so they'll have time to get people excited about what you'll be doing.

Regardless of where you end up, the people in your group are certain to bond in the car as they journey together.

Section Two: Spiritual Growth

The goal of helping young adults grow spiritually should be at the center of your ministry. Ultimately, you want to help them love Christ with their whole hearts, souls, minds, and strength. Only this depth of commitment will allow young adults to live their lives in passionate devotion and service to God.

Section One provided ideas for developing and strengthening relationships with each other. This section focuses on strengthening and deepening relationships with God. Spiritual growth is simple; it's about loving Jesus more and more. But doing that requires spending time with Jesus, praying to him, studying what his Word tells us about loving him, practicing disciplines that draw us nearer to him, and choosing to walk with him every day.

The ideas in this section are like tools. If you leave a tool in a toolbox, it really serves no purpose. But when you use a tool to accomplish a task, you understand that many tools have specific purposes. Use these tools to help the young adults in your group accomplish the specific purpose of growing spiritually.

Growing in Christ

Read John 15:1-17 and the "to know" information in the following paragraph. Then, as a group, talk through the "to discuss" questions. Finally, help everyone remember the quick study by doing the activity in the "to do" section.

To know:

Jesus draws heavily from the Old Testament to present the image of himself as a vine. The vineyard was a symbol frequently used to represent Israel. Sadly, the vineyard was too often unproductive and disappointing to God (see Psalm 80:8-16; Isaiah 5:1-7; and Jeremiah 5:10; 12:10-11). But Jesus announces a new day. He proclaims, "I am the true vine." Whenever Jesus uses the phrase "I am," he reveals something significant about himself as God. As the true vine, Jesus affirms that he is the sole source of spiritual life.

To discuss:

- How do we stay connected to Jesus? What does it mean to "remain" in Jesus, the vine?
- What are key elements of a growing relationship with Christ?
- What keeps people from growing in Christ?
- How has God "pruned" you to make you more faithful?
- What practical things can we do to help us remain in Jesus?

To do:

Distribute paper and pencils or markers. Instruct everyone to draw a tree. It should have five or six branches and fill the whole sheet of paper. (When you hear the groans about drawing, just tell people to do their best.) Group members should write near the tip of each branch something they struggle with in their faith—for example, "too busy for Bible study," "negative attitude," or "tempted with inappropriate sexual relationships." Encourage the group not to look at other people's drawings so no one else sees what each person writes.

Say, "Tear off the ends of the branches containing the things you're struggling with, and put the ends in the trash can I'm passing around." After all the "ends" have been disposed of, divide the group into smaller groups of three to discuss the following questions:

- Think about the things that were tough to write down, or that you were too embarrassed to write. Without revealing specifics, discuss why some of those things are so hard to give up.
- How might getting rid of the things you wrote on those branches help you grow in your relationship with God?

4 Leader Tips on Spiritual Growth

TIP 1

10 Questions to Help You Be a Spiritually Focused Leader

Use the following questions to prepare your own heart spiritually and to help you focus on the essentials as you lead your group.

1. Before God, how am I doing personally?
2. How's my walk with God? Am I up to date with him?
3. Does Christ live in me? How aware am I of that right now?
4. Am I personally prepared to lead?
5. Does my life, in increasing measure, reflect the characteristics of leaders found in 1 Timothy 3:1-7 and Titus 1:5-9?
6. Is there a need, for any reason, to "take myself out of the game" as a leader so I can get right with God?
7. Am I creating an environment in which the "one another/each other" verses of the Bible can be lived out?
8. Am I being sensitive to the Holy Spirit's leading?
9. Do I always keep in mind how I can help each group member grow toward greater Christ-likeness and biblical obedience?
10. Am I praying for each member of our group and the personal needs that come up during our times of prayer?

TIP 2

10 Quick Spiritual Growth Questions

These questions emphasize the fact that even though we're different people, we all share the same faith and all have questions about our faith.

1. How did you become a Christian?
2. What's the most meaningful spiritual experience you've had?
3. What's your relationship with God like right now?
4. What would you like to change about your relationship with God?
5. How do you imagine or picture God?
6. What questions would you like to ask God when you get to heaven?
7. What Scripture passage is most meaningful to you, and why?
8. What confuses you about God?
9. Why did you choose to attend this church?
10. How has your relationship with God changed over your lifetime?

TIP 3

Journaling

Journaling is a great way to facilitate spiritual growth.

Encourage the young adults in your group to journal by providing binders for each individual. Hand out packets of journaling sheets to be included in the binders. Distribute divider tabs with preprinted labels for sections on prayer, Bible study notes, daily quiet time, personal growth, and lessons from everyday life.

Encourage the members of your group to record their prayers for themselves and others, insights from God's word, and any other things God is currently teaching them, on a daily basis whenever possible. Encourage them to bring their journals to all meetings and church services. You can even provide time to write in the journals during meetings.

Needs Survey

Copy the following form, and distribute it to the members of your young adult group. This questionnaire can give you the pulse of where your group is spiritually. Repeat the survey occasionally, perhaps at the start of each ministry "year" so you can adapt what you're doing to best meet the group's needs.

Needs Survey

I would like to learn about (check all that apply)

___ eternal life

___ heaven

___ the Holy Spirit

___ God's attributes

___ the Trinity

___ the fruit of the Spirit

___ Bible history

___ church history

___ what this church believes

___ joy

___ worry

___ contentment

___ trials and hard times

___ pride

___ loving God and others

___ spiritual disciplines

___ fasting

___ what it means to be a church member

___ how to avoid sin

___ what to do about guilt

___ spiritual gifts

___ how to have a relationship with Jesus

___ how to pray

___ how to study my Bible

___ how to take care of myself (nutrition, fitness, skin care)

___ how to build spiritual traditions in my life

___ other: ________________________

Here are some questions I have about God or about being a Christian:

____

____

____

I'd like to study these books of the Bible:

____

____

Here are some needs I have that aren't being addressed in the young adult ministry programs:

____

____

Here are some suggestions for changes and improvements in the young adult ministry at our church:

____

____

25 Spiritual Growth Ideas

IDEA 1
Lent in Any Season

Traditionally, Lent is a time of fasting from Ash Wednesday through Easter. It represents Jesus' 40 days in the wilderness (Matthew 4:1-11). This fasting can take many forms other than refraining from food. When observed with a pure heart, Lent can be a growth experience both personally and corporately. It can also help people sense a strong connection to the body of Christ—past, present, and future.

This tradition of sacrifice and fasting can be a model for any season of submission, prayer, meditation, and discipline. Each individual in the group can choose what to give up, such as TV, Internet use, sweets, or coffee. The idea is to remove those things that distract us from God so we clearly express our need for God and dependence on him.

Discussions throughout this "anytime" Lent, whether in a formal or casual context, can include the following questions:

• Paul describes his suffering with Christ, and his willingness to give up even "good" things for Christ's sake, in Philippians 3:7-11. How are you learning to identify with Christ?

• Jesus exercised self-control when he was in the desert. In 1 Corinthians 10:13, Paul says we will never be given temptation that is too much for us to bear. How can you maintain self-control when faced with temptation?

• How does God fill the void created by the item you're fasting from?

• How does the experience of fasting and sacrifice help you identify with a community of Christians who are also participating in Lent?

IDEA 2

Learning the Holy Spirit's Desires

How can your outlook on life change, knowing that you can trust that the Holy Spirit is working inside you, adjusting and directing your motives, desires, and attitudes?

Often, we focus so much on renewing our minds that we forget that what goes on in our hearts is a deeper and more mysterious process. Our motives, desires, and attitudes are at the core of our actions and lifestyles. It's impossible to force ourselves to want something we don't truly desire or to feel an emotion that just isn't there, but we know that God can change us. Use the following questions to help your group explore the Spirit's role in changing our hearts.

- What is the state of your heart (soft, hard, whole, broken, dark, light)?
- Do you trust God with your heart? Why or why not?
- God changes our hearts through the ministry of the Holy Spirit (Romans 8). As Christians, our hearts have been made new (Jeremiah 31:33; Ezekiel 36:26-27). How can you realize this in your own life?

Break up the young adults into subgroups, assigning each to read a portion of John 14–17. Each group should make a list of everything it observes about the ministry of the Holy Spirit and share these discoveries with the larger group.

Finally, have your group spend time in personal reflection after the discussion. Come together for a time of prayer, asking that the Holy Spirit would align the hearts and desires of individuals in your group with the heart and will of God.

IDEA 3

Openness With God

As Christians, we sometimes feel ashamed about sharing with God the things that weigh heavily upon our hearts, even though we know God is well aware of our deepest secrets. Before the group gathers, create an appropriate atmosphere by dimming the lights, playing quiet music, and giving people the option of having private space.

Read 1 Samuel 1:1-20. In this account, Hannah pours out her heart to the Lord. She serves as an example of someone who was open and unashamed with God. With Hannah's openness and honesty in mind, discuss the following questions:

- What kinds of things do you find most difficult to tell others?
- Why are these topics tough to talk about?
- Do you relate to God as if he's a person or as if he's a thing?
- What are you uncomfortable saying to God? What kinds of things do you avoid telling God?
- What are the benefits of being open with God?
- What holds you back and stops you from being honest with God?

IDEA 4

Corporate Prayer Book

For centuries, Christians around the world have used written prayers in both personal and corporate worship. Written prayers are a way to corporately confess sin, declare the praises of God, and bring requests to him.

Your group can experience prayer in a fresh way by creating a prayer book. Over the course of several weeks, introduce prayer in the context of community. Encourage members of the group to read and study Matthew 6:5-13; John 17; and Acts 2:42.

Ask your group members to write their own prayers. These can be simple, but encourage group members to scan through the Psalms for inspiration. Some individuals might want to follow the pattern of a psalm, some might want to paraphrase and personalize a psalm or other verses that have meaning for them, and still others might be comfortable writing their prayers as poetry or prose.

Ask members of the group to e-mail their prayers to you. Tell them that you'll be deleting names and e-mail addresses, so they can be creative and honest in their written prayers. Make a copy of the prayers for each person in the group. Have your group read the prayers aloud together and then commit to reading them personally every day until your group meets again. If you have a large group, create a concert of prayer by breaking into groups of four or five and having these smaller groups each read aloud a smaller set of the prayers.

IDEA 5

The Sound of Silence

From TVs and radios to CD players and iPods—not to mention cell-phone conversations, barking dogs, and traffic din—noise is a constant in our everyday lives. Yet Zephaniah 1:7 commands us to "Be silent before the Sovereign Lord." First Kings 19:11-12; Psalms 46:10; 62:1, 5; Ecclesiastes 3:7; Isaiah 32:17-18; and Habakkuk 2:20 also link God with silence and indicate that being quiet helps us grow closer to him. Plan a silent spiritual experience for an upcoming meeting to help your group practice the important discipline of silence.

Plan the event for a time the church building will be empty, or set up stations in a room where you can be certain that it will be quiet. (Let the church staff know what you're doing so the group can be undisturbed.) Instruct participants to arrive with their Bibles and be prepared for contemplation.

Set up four stations:

1. a table with chairs pulled up around it, lit with a lamp
2. an area or table with several candles
3. an area or table with a bowl of water, a pitcher of cold water, paper cups, and a wastebasket
4. an area with a wooden shepherd's crook (Check your children's ministry or Christmas pageant costume closet to find one, or make one of your own.)

Place a sign at the front door of the church to direct group members to the room(s) where the stations are set up, and make copies of the handout on page 51. Dim the lights if you can, but make sure group members can still read their Bibles and handouts.

Finally, prepare the "after room" with snacks and drinks. Make sure it's far enough away from the experience room so those who finish early don't disturb the others.

A few minutes before participants are scheduled to arrive, stand outside the experience room to silently greet each person. Give each person a handout as well as a Bible for those who forgot to bring their own. Ask them to follow the directions on the handout and then proceed to the "after room."

When all have finished in the experience room, join them in the "after room." Ask some debriefing questions:

- What was your experience of silence like?
- Did the quiet make it easier to focus on the Bible verses and questions? Why or why not?
- How would your experience have been different if you had read the verses and focused on the objects in a crowded park? in your home?

The Sound of Silence

Please participate in all the stations in complete silence.

1. Enter the room, and sit at the table with the lamps. Open your Bible, and read the following verses: Exodus 14:14-15; Psalms 46:10; 62:1, 5; 131; Isaiah 32:17-18; Habakkuk 2:20; Zephaniah 1:7; James 1:19; Revelation 8:1.

Reflect on these verses. What do they teach you about silence? What role does silence play in your life? Do you need to incorporate more silence in your life? in your relationships? in your prayer practice? If so, how?

Now proceed to the three prayer stations. Listen for the Holy Spirit to teach you about the character of Jesus and his role in your life.

2. Sit at the station with the candles, and look into the flames. Read John 8:12, and reflect on what it means for Jesus to be the light of the world. Think about the concept of light. Have you ever walked in darkness? Does light need darkness to be seen?

3. Proceed to the station with the bowl and pitcher of water. Read John 4:1-14. Dip your fingers into the water in the bowl. Use a cup to take a drink from the pitcher. Think about Jesus as living water. What do Jesus' promises in verses 13 and 14 mean to you personally?

4. Walk to the shepherd's crook, and touch the wood. then read Matthew 18:12-14 and John 10:11-18. Think about how Jesus laid down his life for you. How have you gone astray? In what ways do you feel lost?

When you have finished all the stations, please proceed to ______________________________

____

• Were you distracted by the others in the room? Is it easier for you to pray when you're alone or when you're in a group?

• When you're trying to pray, do you find yourself struggling with outside noise or inner noise? How do you quiet inner noise?

• What does it mean to be silent?

• Why do people link silence and peace?

IDEA 6
Heart Check

Have you ever considered what God's role is when it comes to our personal desires? Do we need to check with God about every little thing? Should we bring God only the "big things" and not bother him with the rest? When are we inviting God into our lives, and when are we just "obsessing"?

Start your time together by handing out index cards and pens. Instruct group members to write down things they do even though they don't "feel like" doing them. Then tell them to place the cards facedown in front of them.

Read this statement by St. Augustine, "Love God and do what you want." Ask, "Can Christians love God and do what they want? Is this what God intends for us?"

Ask for volunteers to read the following verses: 1 Samuel 16:7; Psalms 37:4-5; 51:16-17; Jeremiah 31:33-34; Ezekiel 36:26-27; Matthew 22:37-40; John 14:12-15; Romans 5:5; 8:5.

Then discuss the following questions:

• What are desires?

• Do you think desires are inherently good or bad, or do they depend on circumstances?

• How does God relate to our desires?

• Do you trust God with your desires? Why or why not?

• Duty and desire are sometimes seen as opposites. What place does duty have in our lives when we live by our desires?

Now instruct members of the group to reread what they wrote on their cards. Ask, "Why do you do what you listed on your card if you don't feel like it?"

Ask members of your group to add to their cards during the coming week. They can list activities they don't feel like doing or those they carry through on because they're motivated by guilt. Encourage them to bring their insights to the next meeting to discuss what they've learned.

IDEA 7
Write It on Your Hearts

The Bible, the Word of God, provides not only a way to become stronger in our faith but also to learn more about God's character and to grow closer to him. Deuteronomy 6:6-9; 11:18-21 tells us to write his commandments on our hearts. Joshua 1:7-8 tells us to meditate on God's Word day and night. Colossians 3:16 instructs us to let the Word of Christ dwell within us.

Memorizing Scripture is the first step to fulfilling all these instructions. As we commit God's Word to memory—as we write it on our hearts—amazing things happen. We grow to understand it in new ways, we have access to it at all times, and we can allow it to work within us.

Encourage your group to practice memorizing Scripture by printing relevant Bible verses on index cards. Use a passage from your group's Bible study or verses from your pastor's sermon. Distribute the printed cards to your group members each time you meet.

Encourage group members to place the cards on their medicine cabinets or refrigerators—someplace they'll see them often. Urge them to repeat the verses aloud each day as they brush their teeth or make coffee. Challenge them to quiz each other on the memorized verses.

IDEA 8
The Simple Life

The Bible makes it clear that we are not to store up treasures on earth but in heaven (Matthew 6:19-20). Many verses deal with the problem of possessions: Genesis 14:21-24; Deuteronomy 17:16-17; Ecclesiastes 5:8-11; Colossians 2:20–3:2; Revelation 3:17. Yet many of us fall prey to the concept that the more we have, the better.

One of the great pitfalls of having a lot of "stuff" is that we start fooling ourselves into thinking we can provide for ourselves—that we don't need God. Of course, nothing could be further from the truth.

Challenge your group members to think more about the role of simplicity in their lives with this discussion. At the next meeting of your young adult group or Bible study, look up the above Bible verses pertaining to simplicity and frugality. Ask:

• What do these verses teach about the role of possessions and money in the Christian life?

• What are the dangers of acquiring a significant amount of earthly possessions? Do you find yourself longing for material goods that you don't need? What do you think is behind this longing?

• How would you define biblical simplicity? What's the difference between biblical simplicity and simplicity as defined by magazines such as Real Simple and TV shows such as *Clean Sweep*?

• What place does frugality have in the Christian life? What is its purpose?

• What are some ways we can live lives of simplicity?

Ask the members of your group to quietly and personally consider if any of their possessions are standing in the way of their relationship with God. Do they own items that have become prideful symbols of luxury or status? Do any items clutter their spiritual lives?

Ask group members to choose at least one possession to get rid of and to bring it to your next meeting. At that meeting, collect the items and either donate them to charity or sell them and donate the proceeds to charity.

Finally, lead the group in prayer, asking God to forgive us for looking to our possessions for security rather than to him. Ask God to provide the courage we need to live simply and modestly.

IDEA 9
Walking the Prayer Path

The ancient tradition of walking a prayer path has experienced a renewal recently. The prayer path is a winding path that leads to a central area and then back out again. It's not a maze; rather, all paths lead to the center. Following this path is a way to practice meditation. The Bible calls us to meditate upon God and his works (see Joshua 1:8; Psalms 1:2; 77:12; 119:15-27; 143:5; Philippians 4:8; and Colossians 3:2). One passage in particular is often used as inspiration for walking meditation: "[Isaac] went out in the field one evening to meditate" (Genesis 24:63), which is alternately translated, "Isaac went out in the evening to walk in the field" (New Revised Standard Version).

Find a prayer path, preferably an outdoor one, in your area where you can practice walking meditation with your young adult group. If no prayer path is available near you, you can create your own with *The Prayer Path,* available from Group Publishing (www.group.com).

Prepare your group by reading some of the above passages together. Explain that in a walking meditation, you can pray with both the soul and the body. As you follow the twists and turns of the path, you can reflect on how all the roads in your life have led you to the center, to God. At the same time, you can meditate on God's works as exemplified in nature around you.

Let each member of your group walk through the prayer path at his or her own pace. Afterward, you might want to allow some time for each person to do some journaling about any insights he or she had during the walk. Then debrief with the following questions:

- What was different about praying while walking as opposed to praying while being still?
- How did it feel to pray outside? Has that been a part of your prayer practice before today?
- First Thessalonians 5:17 tells us to "pray continually." Did walking the prayer path give you a better sense of that verse's meaning? Explain.
- Would you walk the prayer path again? Why or why not?

IDEA 10
Overnight Fast

One of the most frequently mentioned spiritual disciplines in the Bible—fasting—is one of the least practiced today. Scripture records that people fasted for a variety of specific reasons: to symbolize repentance and ask forgiveness, to help guide them in making difficult decisions, to ask for God's favor, and even to prepare for battle.

However, the overriding reason to fast is that it helps reconcile us to God. As we deliberately refrain from satisfying our physical hunger, we can reflect on how God satisfies our needs, on how he fulfills us in ways food never can.

Introduce your group to this time-honored discipline by holding your own 24-hour fast. As a group, pledge to fast from Saturday dinner to Sunday dinner. Instead of eating when you normally would, spend time in prayer and looking up Scripture passages about fasting (Deuteronomy 8:2-5; Esther 4:16; Daniel 9:1-3; Joel 2:12-14; Matthew 4:1-2; 6:16-18).

On Sunday evening, break your collective fast by eating a simple meal together. Suggest that group members donate the money they would have spent on meals to an organization that works to eradicate hunger, such as World Vision, Compassion International, or Bread for the World. At your closing meal, talk about what you've learned and the ways you feel closer to God as the result of your collective fast.

IDEA 11
Exprayeriment

Gather your group for an experiment in prayer. Have everyone share the things he or she is praying for, particularly concrete requests (more like "a new job" and less like "peace on earth"). Use a journal to record a list of the prayer requests shared.

Ask if anyone in the group has a favorite faith-boosting Scripture passage about prayer. Read Mark 11:13-14, 20-26. Urge group members to be open and authentic about their experiences of prayer, their level of familiarity with prayer, and their uncertainties about prayer.

Ask those present if anyone would like the group to pray for a specific need at this time. Gather around each person who requests prayer, place hands on that person's shoulders, and pray together for those requests. Use a prayer journal to keep track of how God responds to these specific prayer needs. Sometimes people are surprised and encouraged as they see check marks begin to appear next to the list of requests.

IDEA 12
Christianity and Culture

Spend time as a group analyzing the places where faith and culture cross. Rather than having a movie night, have a movie review night. Ask everyone in the group to bring his or her thoughts on a recent movie (released in the last year) that made him or her think about God, faith, or the church. Discuss how Christianity is portrayed, as well as the world's view of Jesus. Is there a disparity between how it's portrayed in the movie and your own experience?

Have the group give the movies a "thumbs up" or "thumbs down," not based on the quality of the movie but on whether or not the movie accurately portrays the Christian faith.

At a second gathering, discuss a place where Christianity has appeared in another medium (including TV news programs, magazines, or newspapers).

Analyze what image this portrayal of Christianity would give to someone who doesn't attend church. Is it accurate? Is the church generally portrayed in a positive or negative light in these media? Imagine working as a public relations specialist for the church. How could the church go about creating an accurate and positive public image?

A third meeting could focus on images of faith in music. At each of your group's gatherings, discuss how the intersection of Christianity and culture can be opportunities to share the gospel message. How can movies, television, print, and other media create conversations that broach the subject of faith with people who don't know Christ?

Study the passages in Matthew 5:13-16 and Luke 6:22-23, 26. Analyze the pros and cons of developing a positive public image for Christianity. What things do we need to watch out for as we try to do this?

IDEA 13

The Artwork of God

Encourage your group members to collect their favorite or best-known works of Christian art from throughout history. If some of the people in your group aren't art aficionados, they can find many works of art on the Internet. Familiar examples would include Michelangelo's Creation paintings from the Sistine Chapel, the Rose window of the Notre Dame cathedral, and da Vinci's Last Supper. Ask group members to each bring at least one image (a color printout, a book, or a poster).

Not only are pieces of art available online, but analysis of artwork is abundant on the Internet as well. Group members could produce not just an image they're familiar with but also interesting details they find from art critics and students. For example, it was only in the late 20th century that a neurosurgeon looked at the ceiling of the Sistine Chapel with fresh eyes and realized that the shape painted around God is that of a human brain.

Study Philippians 2:1-11. This is believed to be one of the early church's hymns. Then discuss the following:

- What images or themes seem to be most important to the early church?
- Why do you think this was?
- Do they seem relevant or foreign to this generation?

Now discuss the ways faith has been expressed historically.

• What images or themes of faith have been the most important through history? What do you think makes them so important?

• If your group could create a work of Christian art, perhaps to be displayed at your church, what would it look like?

• What themes would be most important to your group?

• What biblical images are most relevant to this generation, and how might members of this group or other Christian artists creatively portray it so a new generation looks at it with fresh eyes?

IDEA 14
The "Rest" of Us

We sometimes hear the words *Sabbath day* when someone reads the Bible in church, but we rarely think of honoring the Sabbath as anything more than going to church.

Spend time together as a group slowing down for a true Sabbath. Take a day off together, and agree to do no work—no e-mail, phone messages, cell-phone calls related to work, or quick trips to the office. Instead, spend the day in a mix of worship and play.

As you start your Sabbath day of rest together, spend some time discussing the following:

• Read Exodus 20:8-11. Why was it so important to God that we spend a day each week in rest and worship?

• Read Psalm 127:1-2. Can you trust together that God will take care of you as you prioritize him over your work?

• Read Genesis 2:8-20. Compare your day of rest to life in the Garden of Eden. How are they similar, and how are they different?

At the end of your day of rest, eat breakfast together (no matter what time of day it is) to celebrate the beginning of a new week. As you chow down, discuss how Sabbath-keeping might become a regular spiritual discipline for you.

IDEA 15
Cross-Cultural Worship

Visit a different church together as a group. Choose a church that features a completely different worship style from what you're used to. Try switching between traditional and contemporary styles, between denominations, or across ethnic and cultural lines. If you belong to a well-established church, visit a new church plant. Look for a congregation of a different age range from your own.

This experience should help you understand spiritually the diversity and depth of the body of Christ. A significant part of spiritual maturity is being able to identify the common elements that bind Christians together and the general differences that are normal within the church.

After church, over brunch or coffee at a nearby cafe, discuss the following:

- What are the similarities and differences between what we're used to and what we've just experienced?
- Are the differences accidental, cultural, or theological?
- Did you find the differences uncomfortable or exciting?
- What can our own tradition learn from the one we've visited?
- Read 1 Corinthians 12. What does it mean to be a "body" together with a group of people who worship in a different way?
- How did we share community with the people we joined for worship?
- Are there any joint efforts or mission projects we could do with this or another church?

IDEA 16
Isaiah Before the Internet

Most young adults probably have a *desire* to spend regular time with Jesus, but they might have a hard time developing this habit. Often it's more a problem of time management and/or priorities than one of commitment. But if it was a priority for Jesus to get away by himself in the morning to pray (Mark 1:35), how much more vital is it for *us* to get regular time alone with God?

Take some time to help group members think through their schedules, looking for pockets of time they could spend with Jesus. Hand out a blank piece of paper to each group member, and have him or her divide the sheet into seven columns, one for each day of the week. Tell group members to think through and write down roughly how they spend their time. This might include the times they wake up and go to bed, work or school schedule, meals, evening commitments, time at the gym, and even TV shows they regularly watch. They can be as specific or general as they would like.

Now have them look for pockets of time that they can spend reading their Bibles, praying, and spending time with Jesus. Perhaps this could happen in the morning during breakfast, during a break at school, or in the evening. It might happen the same time each day, or it might change depending on the schedule. The important thing is to have a plan for each day so other things don't crowd out good intentions.

Another hurdle is that other seemingly important things can easily crowd out our time with Jesus. Ask each group member to identify a daily ritual he or she is certain to do each day. This might be something like reading the morning paper, checking e-mail, or reading a book before bed. Ask group members to consider a one-month commitment to avoid that "daily ritual" until they've spent time with Jesus. No checking e-mail first thing in the morning. No evening novel reading if they haven't spent time praying or reading the Bible yet. At the end of the month, check back to see if group members have noticed a difference in how they view their time and/or their priorities.

IDEA 17

Be a Branch

In John 15:1-17, Jesus gave us a very vivid illustration of spiritual growth and, in doing so, reminded us that *he* is the Vine that we are growing out of and from whom we are to draw our own strength and nourishment as we grow.

Have the larger young adult group break into groups of two or three, and have each smaller group look deeper into this vital passage. Ask your group members to read the passage silently, jotting any notes or questions about things that catch their attention. For example, they might wonder what Jesus means when he refers to "fruit," or they might want to investigate the phrase "apart from me you can do nothing" (verse 5). After five to 10 minutes on their own, have the individuals share their thoughts with the others in their smaller groups.

After another five to 10 minutes, still in your smaller groups, discuss the following questions:

- What does it mean to you that Christ is the true vine?
- What kind of fruit is Christ asking you to bear?
- Do you see evidence of fruit-bearing in your life?
- Can you remember a time God "pruned" you—that is, he cut out some of the dead stuff in your life so you could grow again? What happened?
- What does it mean for you to abide in Christ? Practically, how can you do that? What steps can you take?
- How can you really love others as Christ loved you?
- Who is one person you can love more this week?

Ask the groups to work together on a specific way to apply what they've read and discussed. This could be an action they agree to take. Either individually or as a group project, ask them to identify someone who they really want to work on loving in a Christ-like way during the coming week.

Finally, have the smaller groups close in prayer, thanking God for what he has taught them and asking him to help them apply what they have learned.

IDEA 18
Scribble a Sentence or Two

Journaling is an important skill to develop in order to have a record of where God is taking your group members on their spiritual journeys. While the insight they glean from a morning devotional time seems like it will be a lifetime lesson, chances are that in a few days, it will be difficult to recall the exact verse or insight God used to speak to them.

Share with your group the concept of spiritual journaling—keeping track of lessons they're learning as they regularly spend time with God. They can simply record verses God is using to teach or speak to them, jot down a quote or a line from a song that comes to mind, write out prayers to God, or other ideas. There's no "right" or "wrong" way to journal, and there's not a right number of times per week or month to journal. Some young adults may find it helpful to keep track of what they read each time they spend time with God and perhaps record a key verse for each entry. Others may choose to journal only during extended times with God or only as a way to record their prayers.

Here are some questions group members might want to answer as they journal:

- What did God say to me during my time with him today?
- What verse affected me the most? Why?
- What questions do I have about what I read and studied today?
- What questions would I like to ask God about this?
- What other verses or passages come to mind when I think about this topic?
- What other ideas or images—well-known quotes, music, lyrics, photos, drawings—come to mind when I reflect on these verses?
- What is God asking me to do as a result of this insight?

These questions are less important than being honest about what they're learning, how they feel about it, and what actions they want to take as a result.

One of the most important results of journaling comes in looking back at what God has taught them over the past year (or any period of time). It can be surprising to reread the issues they were struggling with at this time last year only to realize they haven't been problems for months now. And it can be such a joy to see a theme in the verses that God has been using to speak to them for several weeks or months.

IDEA 19

Jesus Said *What* to *Whom*?

Some of your group members may be surprised to learn how Jesus talked and spoke when he was with different types of people. He related to the Pharisees, the crowds, the Jews, and the disciples in very different ways.

The Gospel of John is an excellent book for studying this principle further, but a taste of this idea can be gleaned from studying John 6–7.

Instruct the group members to read these two chapters, asking them to look specifically at how Jesus related to different groups of people. Ask this series of simple questions (you may be able to think of additional questions to get them started):

- What did he say?
- How did he say it?
- Did he explain the meaning of his teachings?
- Did he emphasize grace or truth more?
- What did his relationship with this group of people appear to be?

Ask the members of your group to write down as many of their observations as possible. Allow plenty of time to discuss their findings. Encourage individuals to apply their thoughts in practical ways. The following questions can jump-start their thinking when it comes to application:

- What different types of people do you relate to regularly?
- How can the example of Jesus relating to different groups of people affect how you relate to those around you?
- Are there times God calls you to speak with bold truth? or to speak with large doses of grace and understanding?

Encourage the members of your group to look at other things Jesus said (and who he said them to) with this perspective. They might be surprised what else they can learn from Jesus' interactions with those around him.

IDEA 20
I've Walked in Your Shoes

In 2 Timothy 2:2, Paul encouraged Timothy to pass on the instruction he had received from Paul. Why not provide an opportunity for older members of your church to pass on instruction to the young adults in your ministry?

Create a panel of four to six older Christians. As you think about whom to ask, consider the following questions: Is your group made of mostly singles, young married couples, young families, or a mix of all three? Do you have any single parents? What types of fields do your group members work in? Are there any other unique circumstances?

Look for older Christians in your church who can talk about making it through the stages of life the members of your group are in now. The goal isn't necessarily to have the perfect mix of careers and backgrounds but to have a panel of older Christians who have been walking with Jesus for longer than your group members have. Invite your panel participants several weeks in advance, and have them prepare a short (five minutes or less) account of how they've walked with God through the years. Here are some thoughts to get them started:

- Start with a short description of who you are, for those who might not know.
- Briefly, how did you come to believe in Jesus?
- What did your life look like when you were in your 20s and 30s?
- Are there things you wish you had done differently?
- How did your relationship with Christ affect your relationships with your family, neighbors, co-workers, and friends?
- What advice do you have for those sitting before you tonight?

You might want to go over these testimonies ahead of time to make sure the participants understand what you want them to cover and so they don't go over the time limit.

Once each panelist has shared, you can open up the meeting for questions from your group. Hopefully, your group members will walk away with some new ideas about how they can pursue Christ in their young adult years. And it will be a great encouragement to your panelists to be able to share about their lives with a younger generation.

IDEA 21
The 5 P's of Prayer

Prayer is one of those things that many of us take for granted—to the extent that we aren't always actively pursuing a healthy prayer life. The young adults in your group might have a basic understanding of what prayer is—a conversation with God. But they may wonder how to approach prayer, what to pray for, and how to pray. One simple method of prayer is based on the Lord's Prayer in Matthew 6:9-13.

Walk through the Lord's Prayer together. As group leader, initiate each section of prayer, and allow five to 10 minutes for each section, but leave plenty of room for the Spirit to jump in and direct each section of prayer as well. If things take longer than expected, welcome God's work in your group members' lives.

Praise (Matthew 6:9): Praise God for who he is, for his attributes (he is righteous, holy, just, sinless, good, loving), for his creation, for what he has done, and for what he can do.

Preside (Matthew 6:10): Ask God to rule over your life, the lives of others, and the entire earth. Ask him for his will to be done here as it is in heaven. Pray that both Christians and non-Christians would submit their lives to God's will.

Provide (Matthew 6:11): Ask God to provide for others' needs and for your own needs. This can encompass spiritual, emotional, and physical needs. God wants to meet your needs as well as your desires. John 15:7 says, "If you remain in me and my words remain in you, ask whatever you wish, and it will be given you."

Pardon (Matthew 6:12): Ask God to pardon you from the offenses you've committed against him. Confess the known sin in your life to God. First John 1:9 says, "If we confess our sins, he is faithful and just and will forgive us our sins and purify us from all unrighteousness."

Protect (Matthew 6:13): Ask God to protect you from your own evil desires and from the evil one himself. Also ask God to protect you from falling into temptation. First Corinthians 10:13 says, "No temptation has seized you except what is common to man. And God is faithful; he will not let you be tempted beyond what you can bear. But when you are tempted, he will also provide a way out so that you can stand up under it."

Prayer is the tool God has given us to communicate with him. While there are many different ways to pray, it can be helpful to understand and use the model Jesus gave us to follow.

IDEA 22
Meditation as God Meant It

Scripture meditation is a discipline that easily gets overlooked. Meditation isn't reserved for those following Eastern religions and seeking other gods, nor is it a purely mystic approach to knowing the one true God. Rather, we have the privilege of being able to meditate on the Scriptures God has given us.

Meditation is an inward process that God uses to transform our hearts and minds to look like his. Only as we meditate on God's Word, pondering its meaning and application to our lives, will we discover its transforming power at work in us. Meditation involves more than just reading the Scriptures. It's an intentional reflection, application, and implementation of Scriptures in our lives. This is the process God uses to affect spiritual transformation in our own lives. Romans 12:2 says, "Do not conform any longer to the pattern of this world, but be transformed by the renewing of your mind. Then you will be able to test and approve what God's will is—his good, pleasing and perfect will."

A great passage for the young adults in your group to begin meditating on is Psalm 139. Instruct your group to read through Psalm 139 and then think about (meditate on) the following questions:

- What are your first impressions?
- What words or phrases stand out to you?
- What images do those words or phrases create?
- What are some things God knows about you?
- Do you believe the truths set forth in this passage?
- What is one question you'd like to ask God about what he's teaching you in this passage?

The same questions work for other Scripture passages. Meditating on a Bible passage in the morning can be a great way to stay connected with God for the rest of the day.

IDEA 23

Bible Tool Time

Just as it wouldn't work to build a house if you didn't know how to use a hammer, saw, or screwdriver, it's difficult to study the Bible if you don't know how to use the right tools. While your group members probably know how to read their Bibles, many of them may not know how to dig deeper by using the many Bible reference tools available.

Tell your young adults you'll be having a tool party and you want everyone to bring a favorite tool. Do a skit related to finding the right tool for the job with two men portraying Tim "The Tool Man" Taylor and Al from *Home Improvement* (or two other handymen) to get the group's thinking started.

When tool night arrives, have group members share what tools they brought and why those are their favorites. Then tell them that tonight you'll be talking about *Bible* tools, not building tools. The goal is for each person to also have a favorite Bible tool by the end of the night.

Teaching about these tools will enrich each person's personal Bible study time. You want group members to leave feeling equipped to dig more deeply into the Bible on their own. You'll want to show and explain how to use each of these key tools. The following are just some of the tools you'll want to show your group.

Concordance: An exhaustive concordance lists nearly every word found in the Bible. Different concordances exist for different translations of the Bible. You can look up other verses that have the same key word in them. Exhaustive concordances also list the original Hebrew, Aramaic, or Greek word used, so you can see if the same original word was translated differently into English. Knowing the original word also allows you to look it up in a Bible dictionary.

Bible Dictionary: A Bible dictionary allows you to discover the meaning of many Hebrew and Greek words. Not all words in the Bible are listed in a Bible dictionary. Because several original words can be translated as one English word, it's important to first use a concordance to determine which original language word was used, so you can look up the correct definition.

Encyclopedia of Bible Words: Similar to a standard encyclopedia, this tool can be used to determine the meanings behind Bible words. However, the encyclopedia does not list strict definitions but short articles about the meanings of the words.

Commentary: There are numerous commentaries on the market, ranging from older to more modern. A commentary is one person's or one group's view of the meaning of a passage of Scripture. They can be quite helpful in trying to understand the meaning of a text, but it's vital to keep in mind that it's simply someone's opinion. Different commentaries will have different views on what a verse means. It can be beneficial to look at several different commentaries when trying to determine the meaning of a specific Bible passage.

Topical Bible: A topical Bible is similar to a concordance, in that it lists every verse for a given topic. But where the concordance lists verses based on the actual words in the verse, a topical Bible lists verses by topic. So you could look up the word *hope* and find verses on this topic, categorized into different types of hope. There may even be verses listed that don't include the actual word *hope*.

Spiritual Journal: Think of this as the Swiss army knife among your tools. While all the tools mentioned above have the benefit of thousands of hours of scholarly work and study behind them, don't overlook opportunities to record and reflect on those things that God has spoken to you personally through the Bible and through experiences in your faith walk (see Tip 3 in this chapter for more specific ideas on journaling).

You may have other favorite Bible tools that you'd like to share with your group. The important thing is to start them on their journey in learning how to dig deeper into the Bible on their own. As they leave for the evening, give them a summary list of these tools and how to use them.

IDEA 24
Don't Let Your Quiet Time Be *Too* Quiet!

What is a quiet time? What does the term *devotions* mean? We often use these terms in the church, but not everyone knows what they mean. Take one meeting of your young adult group to go over the basics of spending regular time with God.

Start by explaining the purpose of regular devotions. Read Mark 1:35. Even though Jesus was God, he still needed to get away for time in prayer with the Father.

The key components here are to get away alone and spend time with God. Mornings might work best for some people as a way to start their day right before other things creep in. For others, afternoons or evenings might be better times for them to focus on God's Word. The key is to find a regular time that works for them. Mornings are not more spiritual!

What does it mean to spend time with God? The two big components are reading his Word (what God says to us) and praying (what we say to God). Both of these are important in order to keep this time from becoming a one-sided conversation. God wants to hear *from* us and speak *to* us.

If the idea of a quiet time is new to your young adults (and it will be for some of them), encourage them to start with a small commitment. Perhaps they could choose one chapter of the Bible to read and then spend two to three minutes in prayer. Over time, they'll find that they want to read more of the Bible and spend more time in prayer. There is no magic formula for the perfect amount of time to spend with God. The important thing is that it's genuine.

IDEA 25

Prayer-a-thon

Spending extended time in prayer is a great discipline to teach your young adults. Many prayers occur before meals and bed. It's hard to do much focused prayer during these times. Spending extended time in prayer can be difficult individually but can be encouraging in a group setting.

First, choose a time for your group to join in corporate extended prayer. If this is the group's first experience, a three- or four-hour session on a Saturday is a good place to start. Another option is to do an all-night prayer session from Friday midnight until Saturday morning.

As you plan and promote this event, stress that extended time in prayer doesn't mean four hours of either complete silence or constant talking. Rather, it's a time to explore different forms and expressions of prayer and communication with God.

Break the schedule for your prayer-a-thon into hour-long segments. Then divide each hour into a half hour of reflective time and a half hour of interactive time. A three-hour session could look like the following:

3 p.m.	Corporate praise and worship time (both in song and in prayer)
3:30	Individual confession time
4	Prayer for world missions in small groups of four or five people
4:30	Individual time of thanksgiving, including journaling about what God has done in the past year
5	Specific prayer requests in either small groups or pairs
5:30	Corporate praise and worship again

When broken down into bite-size chunks, a few hours in prayer together can fly by!

Planning an extended time of prayer together might be a great way to celebrate National Day of Prayer (first Thursday of May, www.nationaldayofprayer.org), See You at the Pole (third Wednesday of September—for students to pray together, www.syatp.com), as a closing to a 30 Hour Famine project (www.30hourfamine.org), as a part of a Holy Week celebration, or any time you'd like to get together to pray. What a great way to experience God together!

Section Three: Worship

Can you picture Jesus singing a hymn? The truth is, Jesus lived a life of worship. He honored his Father with his words and actions. For example, he often went off by himself to pray, and just as often he thanked God in front of others.

But sing? For certain, we know how the Lord's Supper ended: "When they had sung a hymn, they went out to the Mount of Olives" (Matthew 26:30). So yes, Jesus knew the importance of worshipping the Father in song.

Early Christians followed Jesus' leading and worshipped God in song. The Apostle Paul told the Christians in Colosse, "Let the word of Christ dwell in you richly as you teach and admonish one another with all wisdom, and as you sing psalms, hymns and spiritual songs with gratitude in your hearts to God" (Colossians 3:16).

Whether or not your young adult group is part of your local church, it is part of the Church with a capital C—the whole body of people who believe in Christ as Savior. As part of the body, be sure you're setting aside times to purposefully carry on the tradition of worshipping God together. The ideas in this section will help your group as you "teach and admonish" and "sing...with gratitude in your hearts to God."

Honest Praise and Open Thanks

Read Psalm 30 and the "to know" information in the following paragraph. Then, as a group, talk through the "to discuss" questions. Finally, help everyone remember the quick study by doing the activity in the "to do" section.

To know:

Thanksgiving psalms and hymns played an important role in ancient Israelite worship. These prayers and songs guided the priests and worshippers of the Old Testament as they expressed their gratitude to and adoration of God. They also teach us important principles of praise and thanks. Praise that pleases God is honest and meaningful, arising from our hearts and minds.

To discuss:

- What actions does the psalmist praise God for?
- What do these actions reveal about God's character?
- What does this imply about the purpose of our praise?
- What does this psalm teach about the act of praise?
- What ingredients are sometimes lacking in your praise or thanks?
- What will be the benefits of offering God your open thanks and honest praise?

To do:

Form groups of four. Give each group copies of several popular praise songs or hymns, a sheet of paper, and a pen. Instruct groups to read their songs and list what the songs say about God. The following questions can help:

- Does this song adequately describe who God is and what he does? Why or why not?
- Do you think this song promotes an attitude of praise? Why or why not?
- In what ways does this song use the ingredients of praise in Psalm 30?
- Based on what you've learned today, can you think of any way you'd improve this song?

3 Leader Tips on Worship

TIP 1

10 Ways to Make Sure Your Worship Is "Right On"

Worship is time to honor, glorify, and exalt God. It's a two-way communication between the Creator and those he created. No matter how small or large your young adult group is, build in times to worship God together. These ideas can lead your group to vibrant praise and worship times:

1. *Prayerfully select the right worship leader(s).* Ask God to lead you to the right person, not just the one with the greatest musical abilities but also one with a heart of worship and the call of God.

2. *Teach about the significance of worship.* The praise and worship segment of your group meetings isn't merely a time of corporate singing. It's turning your complete attention to God, focusing on who he is, what he's done, what he's doing, and what he promises to do. Make sure your group understands the true meaning behind the hymns and choruses!

3. *Yield to the Holy Spirit.* From song selection and preparation to leading and participating in group worship, do it all with a heart that's yielded to God, open to him.

4. *Plan the flow of worship.* Use songs that relate to each another or that focus on the theme of the teaching. Keep things simple—easy to play, easy to sing, with no barriers to worship.

5. *Lead with or without instruments.* A guitar, keyboard, CD or tape, or simply singing *a cappella* all can work just fine. While instruments help with rhythm, they should never be the focus.

6. *Pay attention to openings and closings.* To start, read a meaningful verse or share an inspirational story. To conclude, you might end with a prayer or a call to silence to ponder a particular matter of the heart.

7. Create an atmosphere in which it's OK for everyone to sing. The Bible calls worshippers only to "make a joyful noise," not even necessarily a good one!

8. Allow for personal sharing. If appropriate and as time permits, encourage group members to share something that punctuates the premise of the worship song (for example, for "God Is Good, All the Time," ask, "How has God been good to you this week?").

9. Allow for individual expression. Some group members will raise their hands; others aren't comfortable doing that. Some will sing loudly, others quietly. Be sensitive to the Holy Spirit, and seek to enhance what he's doing.

10. Be alert for spiritual attack. When you desire to live a life that honors and glorifies God, expect spiritual attacks. Pray for God to clothe you with his full armor (Ephesians 6:10-18).

TIP 2

3 Helpful Worship Web Sites

To stay on top of new music and practical helps for worship times in your young adult group, check out these Web sites:

- *www.worshipideas.com.* Free membership gives you access to a weekly newsletter with "tips on building an effective contemporary worship ministry" and much more.
- *www.songs4worship.com.* A one-stop online worship resource with all the latest in praise and worship, plus links to browse music, other resources, music news and views, ministry and leadership, and worship life.
- *www.worshipmusic.com.* The mission of this site is "to increase worship on the earth!" It includes a store for praise music, with titles from Vineyard, Integrity, Hosanna, Maranatha, Worship Together, Hillsongs, and Brentwood, along with "the largest collection of quality independent label worship music."

5 Ways to Make Prayer More Meaningful

Prayer is an important part of worshipping God together—a time to speak to God and to listen for his answers. How can you bring more fulfillment and meaning to the prayer life of your young adult group? Follow these suggestions:

1. *Share answers before you start.* Nothing kindles spiritual fire like knowing God is working in your midst. Encourage group members who've had answers to prayer to talk about those answers with the group. This encourages others that their prayers are worthwhile and assures them that future prayers can be answered just as surely and boldly.

2. *Keep a prayer list.* Urge group members to make their own written lists of prayers. When you pray together, go through the list, and remind the group of items they may have forgotten.

3. *Follow up with each other.* Ask questions about whether specific prayers have been answered. It's important to you, your group, and God that you all know what God is doing in your midst.

4. *Pray big, pray little.* No prayer is too large or too small for God. If something matters to you, it matters to God.

5. *Celebrate answers to prayer.* Have an answered-prayer party to celebrate God's goodness and love in a tangible way. Group members can tell about prayers they've seen answered during the last few months.

20 Worship Ideas

IDEA 1

Body Language

Begin this worship time with songs that mention using our bodies in worship—lifting hands, kneeling, bowing, dancing, or any other way you can think of. During these songs, send several pairs of group members to a different room to work on improvisations. Each pair should create a way to act out one of the following emotions or communications without using words:

- anger
- flirtation
- comforting someone experiencing sorrow
- sharing a joke
- fans at a sporting event

At the end of your music time, have the improv students share their vignettes and ask the audience to explain what they are doing. Ask the gathered group, "What are the easiest things to read from body language?"

Then ask, "What is worship?" In light of the way the group defines worship, ask what an outsider observing one of their worship times—without knowing what it was supposed to be or without being able to hear any sound—would think was happening on the basis of the observed body language?

Ask for volunteers to read these texts one after the other with gusto:

- 2 Chronicles 7:1-3
- Psalm 63:1-5
- Philippians 2:5-11
- Revelation 11:15-17

Generate discussion about these verses by asking the following questions:

- What visions of worship did these texts create for you?
- Why does it seem that people in Bible times were more expressive about their worship than many of us are today? What can we learn from them?

• Do the words and actions we use during worship times match one another? Why or why not?

• When we talk to or about God in "worship," are we stating abstract facts or expressing personal truth? In what ways do you think it's OK to do both?

• How could our young adult group make its worship times more expressive, free, and open to the Holy Spirit's leading?

To close, have the group read Psalm 150 in unison. Leave them with the invitation to boldly express their praise to God!

IDEA 2
Loving God in a Dangerous World

Begin with the question "Where were you and what were you doing when you heard about the attack on the World Trade Center in New York?" As people share their memories, continue the discussion by asking how much time they spent watching or listening to media about the attack that week and why they spent that much time following the coverage of that event.

Then ask the following:

• What were some of the feelings or emotions you experienced right after that event?

• What impact did that event have on your perceptions and attitudes about God?

• At any point during that time, did you wonder, "Is it OK for me to feel these feelings?"

Acknowledge that such questions are part of who we are. The big issue is what we do with feelings like disappointment, anger, and despair.

Recognize with your group that we generally think about praising God when everything is good and we feel safe and prosperous. But God has proven that he is as good as his Word and that he will be there for us no matter how bad things get. No emotion should prevent us from reaching out to God, and the very act of turning to him in our pain, sorrow, and confusion is a sincere form of worship. Together, look at what Scripture says about these emotions. Ask for volunteers to read the following passages:

- despair: Job 7; Psalm 88
- surrender: Job 42:1-6
- helplessness: Psalm 10:12-18

- anguish: Psalm 6
- abandonment: Psalm 22:1-11
- sorrow: Psalm 13
- anger/retribution: Psalm 35:1-8
- worry: Psalm 37:1-8

The more we rely on God in *all* our emotional states, the more we honor him. We can't let trauma or anxiety rob us of our commitments or our confidence in God. Instead, we need to commit ourselves to siding with God and against pain and injustice in every way we possibly can.

Break into groups of two or three. In these smaller groups, discuss how our fears and frustrations with one another can keep us from honoring God. Then share examples of times in life when it seemed God had gone missing but how turning to him and honoring him changed the circumstances.

IDEA 3
At a Crossroads

Point out that there are a lot of different ways to divide people. Demonstrate by asking group members to move about the room as you divide them into a series of smaller groups:

- gender
- rural/urban upbringing
- right-handed/left-handed
- single children/one of multiple children
- arts and humanities majors/science and tech majors/no college and undecideds
- country/rock 'n' roll/rap
- those who pronounce the word *coupons* "coopons"/those who pronounce it "cyoopons"
- dog people/cat people/others
- people who grew up in a church/people who didn't

Instruct them to sit down with the groups they ended with and, in their smaller groups, read Galatians 3:26-28 and then discuss the following questions:

- As you look around your group, what human groups are represented?
- What human divisions are not represented very well at all?

- What differences among people today seem too deep for God to heal?
- What are some possible reasons *this* group isn't very diverse?
- How do you think God wants us to approach divisions in worship?

Instruct each group to brainstorm for five minutes about how your young adult group could become more representative of the larger culture around you. Get the thinking started by looking at different aspects of your young adult ministry.

- Small groups: What types of people are unlikely to get involved?
- Large-group worship times: What can make our gatherings more "diversity friendly"?
- Overall: What fears do we have about reaching out to others who are not like us? What can we gain by reaching out to them?

Outreach and inclusiveness are expressions of praise. What we really like, we tell others about. Close by asking God to give your group boldness to tell others about Jesus, and invite the group to worship God together with you.

IDEA 4
God's Story, Our Stories

Ask volunteers to read the following Scriptures in quick succession. They summarize what you could call "God's biography."

- Psalm 93:1-4
- Genesis 1:1-2, 27
- Genesis 12:1-3
- Exodus 6:2-4
- Leviticus 11:44-45
- Hosea 11:1-4
- Isaiah 9:1-2, 6-7
- John 3:16-18
- Acts 13:32-38
- Acts 17:29-31
- Revelation 21:1-7

God wants your story to be a part of his story. In the same story of rescuing the Jews from Egypt, sending Jesus, starting the church, restoring the church after it got distracted, and raising up missionaries to evangelize the unreached world, God wants to include a chapter about how he transformed your life. It's the story about how you became part of God's love and outreach team for the world. Have you invited him to make your story part of his redeeming story?

Distribute paper and pens, and ask group members to answer the following questions for themselves:

• Who first shared with you about Jesus? Why did they do that?

• Why did the Bible's words about sin and renewal get through to you?

• Who were some of the first Christian "allies" you teamed up with? How have they been influential in keeping you on track?

• As you look around your town and your world, what are some needs you see that you think Jesus probably wants something done about?

Form the young adults into groups of four or five people each. Ask them to "dream aloud" about what their "chapter of God's story" might look like. These questions can get their dreaming started:

• What are the gifts and abilities of those in our group? Which local needs could they help meet?

• What specific qualities of our lives now make it a great time for us to reach out to the world around us?

• What could we do around here and beyond if we decided to?

• What are we going to decide to do?

Close with a time of prayer and celebration, thanking God for including us in his story. Ask him to transform the lives of your group members into significant chapters in his saga of bringing the world back to him.

IDEA 5

God's Story, Our Stories
(Part Deux)

Ask your group members to each remember someone who they considered an important part of their lives when they were in grade school and who they're no longer in contact with. Prod some discussion by asking what happened to the relationship and how they feel about that person now.

The big question is, do we sometimes treat God the same way?

In our relationship with God, we go through several phases. Before we become Christians, we see our stories and God's story as totally separate. Then we move to viewing God's story as something that can benefit our stories occasionally. Eventually, we see our life stories intersecting occasionally with God's story, and we might even want God's story to connect with our stories at some points. We might go through a downtime, when our connections with God's story seem to be part of the past we've left behind. However, God wants our stories to be linked to his story—past, present, and future.

In smaller groups of three or four people, discuss the following as time permits:

• Share about a time you felt closest to God and a time you felt distanced from him.

• Recall a time in the midst of a struggle when God made the best decision obvious to you.

• Give an example of a time you were heartbroken and God brought you comfort, healing, and peace.

• Tell of a time you realized that God could meet the needs of someone you care about and you were bold enough to present that to the other person.

• Admit a time you were so far down that you could barely even pray.

Gather back together as a larger group. Ask for reflections from how the smaller groups answered each question.

Here's the point of this exercise: It might be a surprise—as well as a big relief—to many members of your group that even those not-so-happy chapters of your stories can be part of God's story as well as the good times.

• Read Psalm 107:4-21, and say, "In essence, this passage is saying that being part of God's story won't always feel like being at Disneyland!"

• Read Romans 8:26-28, and say, "What the Bible *does* say is that the Spirit is there to help us, even when we don't know what to ask for, and that God can definitely be at work through all things."

Close with a time of praise, using worship choruses and prayer. Focus on how God specializes in creating purpose where there was only despair, in making wholeness where there was just brokenness, in inspiring joy where there was nothing but disappointment.

IDEA 6
Prayer Centers

Prayer is often the most neglected portion of a church service, yet it is probably the most vital. Scripture is full of beautiful and powerful prayers to God.

Psalm 51—King David wails for kindness and forgiveness.

John 17—Jesus pleads for revealed glory and the disciples' unity.

Acts 12—The apostles' prayers are the vehicle for Peter's deliverance from jail.

Set up different prayer "stations" around the room where your group spends time in worship. Simply gather four or five chairs in a circle or around a table to create each station. Leave room for standing and kneeling, too. If the room is small, you can place the stations around the church building. Each prayer station should focus on a specific theme of prayer, such as confession, thanksgiving, and acknowledging God's greatness.

Place a sign on each station, designating its purpose (such as "Confession," "Thanksgiving," or "Intercession"). Print pages or index cards of Scripture verses that relate to each of the prayer stations, and make those available at the respective stations. For example, the Thanksgiving station might have cards with 1 Chronicles 16:8-36 written out. Isaiah 40 could serve as the passage for God's greatness. Joel 2:12-14, 21-25 would remind readers of repentance at the Confession station. You can also add artwork appropriate to each station, as well as candles, incense, and quiet music to allow for a prayerful mood.

As young adults gather for worship time, encourage each participant to focus on just one station of prayer. This worship activity is designed for individuals to experience God wherever they are in their personal lives. The young adults should approach the stations they choose with the expectation of meeting God there.

IDEA 7
Communal Confession

The confession of sin is a powerful discipline, and when done as a group, its power is magnified even further. During an upcoming group meeting, take time for people to confess sins to one another. Understand that this activity may be difficult for some participants, and proceed with gentleness.

Begin by reading Daniel 9:1-19. Note that while Daniel lived a righteous life before God, he did not have any qualms about confessing the sins of the entire nation of Israel and including his own sins among them while asking for forgiveness. Invite your group members to lift up prayers on behalf of the entire group and your church, confessing where you have collectively fallen short before God and asking for his forgiveness and help for your group or church to improve in those areas or even to make restoration where needed.

Then read Romans 2:1-4. Remind your group of Christ's death for the sins of the world and of Christ's kindness that leads us to repentance. At this time, ask your group to split up into pairs to confess their sins to one another. The sins confessed don't need to be sins against someone in the group. The point of this activity is to experience the process of forgiveness through the admission of sins. However, encourage your group members to also seek out those in the group they may have wronged if they need to ask forgiveness.

The length of time will be discretionary, knowing that some will choose to confess to more than one person and some to only one or none. Give the option to confess to God privately if some feel awkward. Those who hear confessions should extend grace to those who confess.

Stress that this activity isn't meant to create additional guilt within those who confess. Rather, it's designed to create an atmosphere of forgiveness and freedom from sins. Forgiveness is powerful. This experience will build bonds between those in Christ.

Close with a group reading of the Lord's Prayer (Matthew 6:9-13).

IDEA 8

Interpretive Reading

Place a number of microphones throughout your group's worship area. If the room you use is small, you might not need to use amplification. Invite those attending to go to a microphone and read a portion of Scripture they've been meditating on or feel is a powerful passage. The goal is to allow God to speak to your group through the Bible in a fresh way.

Encourage those who read Scripture to do so interpretively. They can rework the passage in their own words, act out the verses, or even read expressively for a modern translation or paraphrase. The idea is to allow the ancient text to feel new and alive and to remind worshippers that God's powerful Word changes lives.

You can announce this activity a week before it takes place so young adults can meditate on certain passages of Scripture, study the context and background for greater insight, recast the passage into their own words, or find alternative contemporary translations.

IDEA 9

Celebrating the Lord's Supper

The Lord's Supper is a sacred time for the church. It is also a time that allows worshippers to experience a multisensory commemoration of Jesus' death and resurrection. While churches celebrate the Lord's Supper in different ways, the goal of this activity is to create an experience similar to what first-century Christians observed.

Set up tables at the front of the room for the elements. Instead of using loaves or pieces of leavened bread, put out unleavened matzo bread. (This bread can be purchased at any store that carries international or kosher foods.) Wine or a nonalcoholic substitute is discretionary. Position candles, artwork, and icons depicting the death and resurrection of Jesus around the bread and wine.

Unleavened bread is a symbol of the Israelite's exodus out of Egypt. Read Exodus 12:14-27, and remind participants that Israel had been enslaved by Egypt for 400 years before God miraculously delivered the Israelites from oppression. Israel left Egypt so quickly that the bread didn't have time to rise. That is what unleavened bread is. The matzo provides an image of God's deliverance.

Likewise, the Passover feast reminded Israel of the price paid for their deliverance: blood. God's requirement that an unblemished male lamb be sacrificed foretold the greater sacrifice and complete deliverance that Christ's death on the cross accomplished. Christ's sacrifice set us free from the oppression of sin.

Now read Mark 14:22-26. As Christians, when we partake of the Lord's Supper, we mark Jesus' death and resurrection. And we retell the story of Jesus to recognize his role as the true Passover lamb. Break the matzo bread as a visual reminder of Christ's broken body. Spill or pour out some of the cup as a reminder of his spilled blood.

Invite the worshippers to proceed to a table to take the elements when they're ready. Encourage people to celebrate together—as couples or together with three to four close friends.

IDEA 10

Meditation on the Lord's Prayer

While many of us read the Bible, very few of us really meditate on God's word. Meditation is the practice of giving your mind to a single thought or idea. For Christians living in a world marked with overstimulating images, meditation is key to fixing our minds wholly on the Lord. Paul reminded the Christians in Colosse to set their minds on the things above and not on the things of this earth (Colossians 3:2). Meditation is a way to give our minds and imagination to God instead of the world.

In a worship gathering of your young adult group, recite the Lord's Prayer (Matthew 6:9-13) together. Be sure the room is still and quiet—no music. Lighting should be minimal, just bright enough to read the verses. Light candles or burn incense as a reminder of our offering of prayer as a sweet scent to the Lord.

After you've read the prayer in unison, have individuals read the prayer one verse at a time. Ask worshippers to quietly meditate on each verse for a few minutes. This shouldn't be a time of aimless daydreaming but a time of extended concentration on the Lord and his magnificent words. At first it might seem difficult to remain on just one thought, but ask the Holy Spirit to calm your thoughts and to help you be attentive to Scripture. Encourage the group to listen for words and phrases that pop out at them, and ask them to briefly share those words at the end of each period of meditation.

After working your way through all the verses, recite the prayer in unison again.

IDEA 11

Mosaic Worship

In the area where your young adult group will gather for your worship service, set out art supplies such as poster board, colored paper, paint, clay of various colors, colored glass, and grout. Start by asking the group members what past experiences they have had with art or artistic expression, whether creating their own works or simply looking at others. Discuss how the passions and talents of artists influence us individually as well as the whole world.

Read the story of the artist Bezalel together in the passages below (try using *The Message*). Focus on how this story shows people using their gifts and skills to honor God. These specific verses provide great insight into God's pleasure from this sort of creative worship, as well as what people get out of it:

- Exodus 31:1-11
- Exodus 35:30–36:7
- Exodus 37:1-9
- Exodus 39:32-43

Now ask group members to discuss their own God-given gifts and passions, using these questions as a guide:

- What are your unique gifts, skills, and artistic talents?
- How do your gifts affect others and your world?
- How can you worship God with the creative passion and talents he has given you?
- What do we get out of honoring God artistically and with our gifts?
- In what ways can we worship God with art?

As you continue in a quiet and meditative mood, work together to create a mosaic. Use clay, paper, or pieces of glass. Each person should contribute something to the piece of art as a worship offering to God. You might encourage people to paint or write words of praise on their individual pieces or to find other ways to make pieces uniquely theirs.

To close, discuss how the creativity and artistic talent of individuals in the group combined to form something greater than the individual pieces. Discuss how that relates to worshipping together, and then discuss how the mosaic reflects the beauty of our worship to God.

Bonus idea: If you have time, go to an art museum or exhibit together before creating the mosaic. This experience will smoothly lead young adults into contemplation of gifts and art and will spark creativity as you go about making your own worshipful art.

IDEA 12
The Honor Journal

Instead of praying or singing aloud together, during this worship time, your group will express worship to God by journaling. However, there will be just one journal that will travel around the room so young adults can take turns writing in it. (As an alternative for a large group, you can provide several journals and form several smaller groups.)

Set a comfortable mood by playing reflective music in the background. No guidelines exist, except that each person will journal his or her worship and pass on the book to someone else. Each person can write a phrase or a paragraph, in the form of a poem, a letter, or a song to God. Some may choose to do drawings. If someone seems stuck, he or she might copy a favorite Scripture verse into the journal and add some reflective thoughts.

People who aren't writing in the journal should spend time connecting with God however they'd like; ideas include reading Bibles you've scattered around the room or just being silent and reflective. Encourage them to be quiet and not be a distraction to anyone else. After everyone has had the journal, read aloud your worship together, offering it to God once again.

IDEA 13
Total Surrender

Encourage your group members to surrender their everyday lives and choices to God. Ask everyone to find an object that represents an area that prevents him or her from genuinely worshipping God. Group members can find something in the room or take something out of their bags, pockets, wallets, or purses.

For example, individuals might choose a cell phone, a laptop computer, a photo, a watch, or a running shoe. Provide extra objects for people who don't have anything to choose from.

Say, "Hold the object in your hand. Offer it to God in prayer, asking him to take away the distractions in your life and to help you sincerely worship him. After you've prayed, place the object on the floor as a symbol of surrendering your life to God and committing to worship him with your whole heart."

After everyone has prayed individually and placed his or her object on the floor, read Psalm 9:1-2 aloud. If you want to read a longer passage, choose Psalm 73:23-28. Close in prayer, asking God to help all of you worship him completely and sincerely, without distraction.

IDEA 14

Intimate Silence

Set up two or three experience stations that can help young adults focus on God in silence. Remind the group that the silence isn't just for the sake of being quiet; silence is a spiritual discipline that leads us to a more intimate relationship with God. Turning away from the noise of our busy lives and embracing silence is a way of worshipping God.

There should be no talking or other noise that would distract people during this time. Instruct group members that they can visit any of the stations in any order and spend as much time at each as they want. The purpose of these experiences is to focus on God and listen closely to God's "still small voice" (1 Kings 19:12, King James Version) that they aren't as able to hear in the chaos of their everyday lives.

Here are the stations:

Station 1: Put out a bag of disposable earplugs; a wastebasket; and several cushions, pillows, and blankets for people to sit on.

Include the following instructions on a card at this station: "Put a set of earplugs in your ears, close your eyes, and spend a few minutes simply listening to God. Try to clear your mind. This isn't a time to mentally sort through your to-do list or even to throw out your prayer requests; rather, the goal is to come before God with a still heart and mind and receive the peace, encouragement, message of love, or Scripture that he wants to give you."

Station 2: Set out a lit candle for each participant.

Include the following instructions on a card at this station: "Spend time in prayer, silently offering a prayer of thanksgiving to God. When you've finished, blow out one of the candles. Watch as the smoke rises—the rising scent and smoke represent your prayers rising to God. Even though you haven't spoken any words aloud, God hears and receives your prayers."

Station 3: Provide Bibles, notebooks, and pens or pencils. With sticky notes, mark in the Bibles several passages that explore authentic worship of God: Psalms 63:2-3; 95:6; John 4:23-24; Romans 12:10-13; Ephesians 5:19-20; Philippians 2:9-11; Hebrews 13:15-16; James 4:7-10; Revelation 4:8-11.

Include the following instructions on a card at this station: "Read the marked Bible passages or another that you choose on your own. Use the paper and pen to express the meaning of that passage in your own way. For example, you can draw yourself drawing near to God, write a summary in your own words of the passage you've read, or write a worshipful prayer to God based on the passage. It's up to you how to connect with God through the Bible."

Incorporating silence into your worship time will strengthen relationships with God and bring rest and renewal to tired spirits.

IDEA 15

Lectio Divina

Lectio divina is an ancient form of meditation on Scripture in which an individual or group reads a passage of Scripture slowly and repeatedly until a word or phrase pops out for the reader or readers. It is a simple but powerful way to worship God through Scripture. In this activity, the group will read Romans 5:1-11 aloud three times together. Encourage them to listen very carefully to the brief instructions you'll provide before you read the verses together each time. Be sure to read the passage carefully so the group will be able to absorb it.

Before you read the passage together the first time, say, "As we're reading this passage for the first time, focus on the meaning of the phrases and words you are saying."

Before you read the passage the second time, say, "As we read the passage again, focus on acknowledging God's holiness and omnipotence and worshipping God with love."

Before reading the passage together the third time, say, "As we read the passage this last time, focus on letting the truths of God's Word impact your hearts and minds."

After the three readings, set out bowls of water. Finish the worship experience by guiding individuals to dip their hands into the water. Discuss how God has cleansed us from our sin through Jesus' death and resurrection.

Other passages that would work well for a *lectio divina* worship experience include

- Luke 7:36-50
- Luke 18:18-30
- Colossians 1:15-23

IDEA 16

Good Friday Food and Fellowship

Invite the young adult group to have fun making a traditional English Good Friday treat—hot cross buns. These rolls are easy to bake, and the end result tastes a bit like warm cinnamon rolls. It doesn't even have to be Good Friday for your group to try this activity.

Preparing and eating food may not seem like a typical way to worship. After all, it doesn't involve prayer or singing. But throughout Scripture there is a connection between food and worship—from the original Passover celebration to Jesus' Last Supper with his disciples.

Eating hot cross buns as a Good Friday tradition dates back several hundred years. Some historians believe hot cross buns were eaten to commemorate Christ's death as early as the 12th century. For Christians who eat this food on Good Friday, the cross shape cut into the top of the roll signifies and celebrates the significance of the day: the death of Christ on the cross and the price he paid for our sins.

As you work together to prepare the hot cross buns, invite participants to partake of the texture, smells, and labor of kneading the dough with the same focus they'd have if they were singing a worship song or meditating on God's goodness.

Making the rolls will take about two to three hours, depending on the recipe you select and the time needed for the dough to rise. Many standard cookbooks contain recipes for hot cross buns; you can also find recipes online.

While the rolls bake, take time to discuss the meaning of Jesus' death by inviting participants to share what Good Friday means to them. Use the following questions to get your discussion started:

- Should Good Friday be treated in sorrowful remembrance or in celebration? Why?
- What Scripture passage is particularly meaningful to you as you celebrate Good Friday? Why?
- How has Jesus' death affected your life?
- As we marked the rolls with a cross, how is your life marked by the cross and the events of Good Friday? Do others see it? If so, how?

IDEA 17

Hymn Revamp

Bring new life to old hymns by using them to prompt creative writing and prayerful meditation. Select a hymn with especially meaningful lyrics such as "When I Survey the Wondrous Cross," "Great Is Thy Faithfulness," or "And Can It Be That I Should Gain?"

(Note: Although many hymns are public domain, it is important to check beforehand. If necessary, your church can obtain a license from Christian Copyright Licensing International (CCLI) for a small fee. Visit www.ccli.com for more details.)

Hand out copies of the hymn lyrics as well as paper and pens, and then prompt participants to spread out around the room and read the lyrics on their own. Direct young adults to respond to the hymn in writing, such as rewriting the stanzas of the hymn in their own words, composing poetry centered on the themes of the hymn, or journaling personal reflections about a line that most directly speaks to their spiritual journey. Play reflective instrumental music in the background while participants are writing.

After 10-30 minutes of writing, gather the group back together, and invite volunteers to read selections from what they wrote. Conclude by leading participants in singing the hymn together. After this experience, that "old" hymn will never be the same.

IDEA 18

Multilingual Praise

Develop a sense of connection with the worldwide body of Christ by infusing a multilingual element into your group's worship service. Ahead of time, invite group members who are proficient in other languages to prepare Scripture readings in those languages. Suggest texts such as Psalms 67; 117; Philippians 2:5-11; Revelations 5:9-10; 7:9-10.

Create a handout for participants, including those who don't know anything beyond "Adios!" "Sayonara!" or "Aloha!" For the handout, translate the phrase "We worship you, Almighty God!" into several languages. Use foreign language dictionaries, people who speak other languages, or language translation Web sites such as world.altavista.com, www.freetranslation.com, or translation.langenberg.com. List this phrase in eight to 10 different languages on the handout, and be sure to include pronunciation clues when needed.

When you gather to worship, begin by reading John 3:16, and then say, "God loves *the world*. It's easy to forget that we're part of a global church! We're worshipping Jesus alongside brothers and sisters in Christ who we've never met but with whom we have a common eternal bond."

Invite participants to present their prepared Scripture readings while others follow along in their English translations. Then lead the group in a responsive reading of the phrases on the handout. Shout, "We worship you, Almighty God!" and have the group respond by repeating what you said. Once they get the hang of it, shout the phrase in the first language on the handout, with the group responding similarly by repeating after you. Continue reading through the various translations on the handout, and then conclude by shouting in unison, "We worship you, Almighty God!"

IDEA 19
Sacred Solitude

We all long for time alone with God, yet we all struggle with the discipline required to carve out that sacred time during busy and stress-filled days. Schedule a mini-vacation with God for the young adults in your group by inviting them to gather for four hours as a group.

Instruct them to bring Bibles, journals, a blanket, a portable CD player and worship music CDs (optional), a Christian book (optional), a jacket (if needed), and pens. Meet at a scenic location with plenty of room for participants to go safely on a walk alone or find private space.

Say, "Matthew records a very important habit that Jesus had: spending time in solitude with the Father. Matthew writes that after Jesus miraculously fed the 5,000, 'Immediately Jesus made the disciples get into the boat and go on ahead of him to the other side, while he dismissed the crowd. After he had dismissed them, he went up on a mountainside by himself to pray. When evening came, he was there alone' (Matthew 14:22-23).

"Like Jesus, we can benefit greatly by stepping away from the crowds, demands, and hectic schedules of our lives. Today we're going to spend some extended time with God, and with God *alone.*"

Then take a few minutes to explain the premise. Participants will spend three hours alone. That's right, *three hours!* During this time, they should focus on God's presence and evaluate how they're doing on their spiritual journey. A couple of simple questions might help them focus:

- What are your goals for spiritual growth?
- How has God been faithful to you over the past year?

Group members can also spend time worshipping God, praying aloud, or with him in silence. They also may want to spend time reading Scripture, taking in-depth study notes, or meditating on meaningful verses.

Give them an honest warning: It will be challenging for most of them to spend three hours alone with God. We all get so used to media stimulation and interaction with others that we're likely to have a sense of discomfort with solitude. Assure them that it's OK to feel that way, but encourage them to take on the challenge with a sense of determination and expectancy.

Arrange a place and time to meet at the end of the three hours, and then gather back together. Sit in a circle, and invite participants to share about what they experienced during their time of sacred solitude. Use the following questions to think through the experience:

- How easy or hard was it for you to focus on God? Why?
- How did God speak to you?
- What observations did you make about your spiritual life?
- What did you observe in nature that was meaningful to you?
- How did it feel to simply slow down and spend time doing nothing?
- How can you incorporate regular times of silence or solitude into you daily habits?

If young adults find this time spiritually helpful and emotionally refreshing, schedule similar mini-retreats regularly during the year.

IDEA 20

Vertical Stories

Create a visual reminder of God's faithfulness and his love for every group member with this simple activity.

Ahead of time, cut white paper into approximately 4x11-inch strips (by cutting letter-sized paper in half vertically). Also, collect a variety of colored markers.

Hand out two paper strips and a marker to each young adult. Invite group members to spend time reflecting on their own spiritual journey. The following questions can help:

- When did Jesus first become real to you?
- How have you grown in faith over the years?
- What have been the important "landmarks" along your spiritual journey?
- How has God been faithful to you?
- How has God been speaking to you recently?

Ask participants to use markers to record their faith stories in a vertical column on the two paper strips. They should try to fill both strips with their personal reflections and can use additional paper strips if needed.

After about 15 minutes of writing time, have participants exchange paper strips with each other so they can read about others' faith journeys. If time allows, have group members continue to exchange papers until they've read several different faith stories from members of the group.

Spend some time praising God together for the variety of ways he has worked in people's lives. Invite participants to share what stood out to them about God's faithfulness as they read each other's stories. Talk about what it means to be a community of faith.

Finally, have the group members use tacks or tape to affix the strips horizontally along the wall of the room where you're meeting to create a wallpaper border. Keep the border posted on the wall for several months as a testimony to God's faithful work in each person's life.

Section Four: Bible Studies

Bible studies are at the core of young adult ministry. This section contains eight ready-to-go Bible studies that you can use with your young adult group. (In addition, you'll find a Quick Study that will help your group understand the importance of studying the Bible and tips on leading Bible studies.)

Each of the eight ready-to-go Bible studies—which begin on page 103—includes a primary Scripture passage that you'll read, along with a section of background information that will help young adults see how the Scripture relates to people today. Next is a Bible exploration and application section, which will help your group actively and interactively dig into the Scripture passage and apply the teachings to their own lives. Finally, each study includes a closing to help young adults remember what they've learned and to commit to each other and God to make changes based on the study.

Feel free to adapt these studies to your group's needs. Add or delete questions or Scripture passages. (A complete list of the passages used in these studies is included at the end of this chapter.) Change the activities or closing prayer times to fit your group.

Most important, enjoy what your group learns through these studies, and use them to help your group grow closer to God and understand their relationship with him better.

Tested Against God's Word

Read Acts 17:11-12 and the "to know" information in the following paragraph. Then, as a group, talk through the "to discuss" questions. Finally, help everyone remember the quick study by doing the activity in the "to do" section.

To know:

Paul's preaching in Berea was primarily to Jews. These Jews may have heard of Jesus, but they apparently had never heard the full message of Jesus. While the Bereans received Paul's message eagerly, they also tested it against the Scriptures.

The message that Paul preached to the Bereans was the same message he had preached to the Thessalonians a few days earlier. He explained to them, using the Old Testament Scriptures, that the Messiah they'd been waiting for had to suffer and rise from the dead. Then he proclaimed to them that Jesus was that Messiah (Acts 17:2-3; for a more complete example of Paul's message, see Acts 13:16-41).

The Bereans did three good things: they listened to Paul with open minds; they checked Paul's message against Scripture to see if it was true; and upon discovering the truth, they accepted it wholeheartedly. They were neither too skeptical to consider the message of Christ nor too naive to accept any message without checking it against God's Word.

To discuss:

- What wisdom did the Bereans gain from examining the Scriptures?
- How is our searching for answers in the Bible similar to the Bereans' examining of the Scriptures?
- Why do you think the Bereans were eager to examine the Scriptures?
- How does our eagerness to study the Scriptures compare to the Bereans' eagerness?
- How can we be more like the Bereans in our outlook on the Bible?

To do:

Divide the group into trios. Instruct the groups of three to find out things they don't already know about their group members by asking questions. (No one has to answer a question he or she feels uncomfortable answering.) If the trios have trouble getting started, suggest a topic such as careers, dreams, or fears. Then, with the whole group, discuss the following questions:

- How did you feel about the answers you received to your questions?
- What did you discover by asking questions?
- How does the way you searched for information about each other compare with the way we search for answers in the Bible?
- What can we learn about studying the Bible from this activity?

Leader Tips

4 Leader Tips on Leading Bible Studies

TIP 1

Bible Study Plan

Whether your group uses a traditional Bible study resource, makes use of the Bible studies in this section, or does something wild and crazy like studying while hang gliding or snowboarding, the main thrust of a Bible study is the study and teaching of the Scriptures.

As leader, you could take a teacher approach, but you might enjoy the time more if you think of yourself as a facilitator—someone who keeps the discussion generally on the right track but who doesn't need to fill the time with the sound of your own voice. In fact, you might challenge yourself to listen to what other members of the group can teach you.

Part of keeping your group "on track" is having a plan. Here's one agenda you can follow—while, of course, allowing for flexibility if the Holy Spirit has something new in mind for your group.

10 minutes—Welcome. Use this time to check in and catch up with each other.

20 minutes—Worship. A time of corporate singing to focus on who God is, what he's done and is doing, and what he's promised to do. This can be led by a group member or team (depending on your Bible study/small group's size). Be flexible and creative, and use simple instruments or a worship CD. The goal is to prepare group members' hearts to receive God's Word.

45 minutes—Bible study and discussion. As you facilitate the discussion, be sensitive to God's leading. Keep in mind that the goal of effective Bible study isn't gaining knowledge for the sake of knowledge. Rather, the goal is life change—applying biblical truth in your everyday lives.

15 minutes—Prayer. Spend time sharing prayer requests, sharing reports of answered prayer, and lifting each other and your requests before God.

30 minutes—Fellowship. While this can be an optional time and group members can leave if necessary, stress to your group that getting to know each other is a vital part of growing in your faith.

TIP 2

5 Creative Ways to Approach Bible Study

Here are some ways you can take age-old truths and a few ancient practices and apply them in fresh ways in the 21st century.

1. *Deepen Scripture's meaning through metaphor.* The Bible describes God as the shepherd, rock, fortress, Living Water, Bread of Life, Fire, and Wind, to name just a few. When studying a passage that portrays God with imagery, use that metaphor in your lesson. You'll be surprised how well people remember the main idea of a study when they have an image to associate it with.

2. *Send summary reflections.* Send a digital summary via e-mail to help group members remember the main ideas from your study. Add questions for further reflection, and give a preview of what you'll be studying during the next lesson.

3. *Picture it!* Use images to help people learn and remember the main ideas of your lessons. Before meeting, read your passage, record the emotions and reactions the text creates, collect images that affect you in a similar way, and integrate those images into your lesson.

4. *Awaken minds by using hands.* Distribute small pads of paper and a can of Play-Doh, and invite people to draw and mold away during the lesson. You may be surprised how some people come alive with new insights through using their hands!

5. *Divide into subgroups for discussion.* Some people process information best through interacting with others. Divide into subgroups of three or four (depending on the overall group's size), and give specific questions to discuss. Then come together and share your answers.

TIP 3

5 Ways to Live Out What You're Learning

If your young adult meetings include a Bible study, you may discover that people sometimes leave without ever really understanding how to apply what you've been studying. Here are some activities that can be paired with a study to help members of your group make those connections:

1. *One verse.* Choose one verse of Scripture—perhaps a meaningful verse or short passage from your Bible study—that your group agrees to study and meditate on throughout the coming week. Each person should study the verse, reflect on its meaning, and pray it to God, focusing on the verse several times a day. When you meet again next week, group members can share what God is teaching them.

2. *One hour.* As a group, commit that for the next week, you'll all surrender one hour daily that you'd typically spend watching television or reading a book. Instead, spend that hour quietly with God each day. Each person should make notes about what God is teaching them and then share what he or she is learning when the group next meets.

3. *Creative thanksgiving.* Before members of your group head their separate ways this week, form groups of two or three, and have each pair or trio express thanks to God by writing a poem or song, drawing a picture, or creating a skit. Each pair or trio can then present its project to the rest of the group.

4. *Words of encouragement.* Before you dismiss your group, take turns showering each other with words of encouragement. Sit in a circle, and select someone as the person to be encouraged. Have group members each say something encouraging to the person. The "encouragee" isn't allowed to speak or respond to any comments. After everyone has had an opportunity to share, select another person to be encouraged. Repeat the same process for everyone in the group.

5. *Party time.* Plan a celebration of joy—a party! Ask each group member to bring and share a favorite party food; favorite upbeat praise music; and at least five favorite clean jokes, funny stories, or cartoons.

TIP 4

3 Vital Questions Before You Lead a Study

Whether you or someone else leads the Bible studies of your young adult group, the leader's job is to act as a discussion facilitator, not a preacher. Spend some time thinking about how the Bible passages your group is studying relate to your own spiritual growth. Answer the three questions below, and you'll have all the material you need for generating discussion. Others in your group will feel free to contribute their own insights, comments, and questions in response.

1. What experience in my own life confirms or conflicts with the verses in this study?

2. What themes or statements in these verses stand out to me as most important, significant, or controversial?

3. What questions, comments, insights, and personal applications flow from this material for me that I can share with the group?

How Can I Know God's Will? STUDY 1

Read John 10:1-6, 24-30. Then read the background information to see how the passage relates to people today.

Background Information

In John 10:1-6, 24-30, Jesus teaches that his sheep listen to his voice and follow him.

Jesus wasn't the first to refer to God's people as sheep. Moses, for example, asked God to appoint a leader so God's people wouldn't be like sheep without a shepherd (Numbers 27:17). Ezekiel used the sheep metaphor to discuss Israel's total dependence on God, the only completely reliable shepherd (Ezekiel 34). So Jesus was using a well-known image when he spoke of his followers as sheep (see also Psalms 95:7; 100:3).

The sheepfold that Jesus mentions was a closed pen made of stone walls, with an opening in one of the walls. It could be located in the hills where the sheep grazed or beside the house of the sheep's owner. In either case, the sheep pen's primary function was to protect the sheep during the night. Each morning the shepherd would call each sheep by name and lead the flock out to pasture.

Jesus makes a couple of points with the sheep metaphor. First, he alone is the true shepherd. The Jewish religious leaders who oppose him (John 9:13-34) are little more than bandits and thieves.

Second, we must listen for Jesus' voice and follow him. Jesus won't permit us to hide within the walls of the sheep pen. He asks us to follow him out into the world. Our responsibility, according to John 10:27, is to listen carefully for Jesus' voice and follow wherever he leads us.

Bible Exploration and Application

Before your group meets, make a photocopy of the "They Say..." handout on page 105 for each member of your group. Have participants form groups of four people, and give each person a copy of the handout. Tell groups to read and follow the instructions at the top of the handout.

Once group members have completed and discussed the handout, discuss the following questions in the larger group:

- Which of the quotations do you think best describes the nature of God's will? Explain.

- What do the quotations reveal about people's understanding of God's will?

Say, "As the quotations and our discussion reveal, people have different perspectives about God's will. However, the most important thing about following God's will is knowing God and recognizing his voice. To discover what this means, read John 10:1-6, 24-30 in your groups."

Then have group members discuss the following questions:

- How are we similar to the sheep Jesus describes? How are we different?
- What are the responsibilities of the sheep? of the shepherd?
- To what extent can we know where our shepherd is leading us?
- What things keep us from hearing Jesus as well as we could?
- What's one thing Jesus may be calling you to do today?

Come back together as a larger group to discuss your answers. Afterward, say, "God's will doesn't have to be intimidating. We simply need to remember that we're following a person, not a plan, and that following God's will means following God."

Closing

Form a large circle, and say, "We've explored how following God's will means following God. But it takes wisdom to know how to follow God. Let's close in prayer, asking God to give us the wisdom to follow him in the situations we face every day."

Close with the following prayer, inviting group members to take turns completing the middle section with brief prayers. Pray, "Dear God, we want to follow your will, but sometimes we don't know how or where to find it. Help us know how we can follow you in these specific situations. Help me as I..." (Complete the sentence, and invite group members to do the same by naming specific situations in which they're seeking God's wisdom.) "Thank you, God, for promising to lead us where you want us to go. Help us confidently follow you and your will with each choice we make. In Jesus' name, amen."

They Say. . .

In your group, read the quotations below, discuss what each one says about God's will, and explain why you agree or disagree with the statement.

1. "We do not know the play. We don't even know whether we are in Act I or Act V....We are led to expect that the Author will have something to say to each of us who has played. The playing it well is what matters infinitely."—C. S. Lewis

2. "A possibility is a hint from God."—Søren Kierkegaard

3. "If a man will begin with certainties, he shall end in doubts; but if he will be content to begin in doubts, he shall end in certainties."—Sir Francis Bacon

4. "He who works for sweetness and light united, works to make reason and the will of God prevail."—Matthew Arnold

STUDY 2

Where Do I Begin?

Read 2 Timothy 3:14-17. Then read the background information to see how the passage relates to people today. Also be sure to have several sheets of newsprint available, as well as a pack of 3x5 cards and enough pencils to give out to group members during the study.

Background Information

In 2 Timothy 3:14-17, Paul encourages Timothy to hold fast to what he's learned from God's Word.

At times, searching for God's will for our lives may leave us frustrated and uncertain. Unsure of exactly where God is leading us or precisely what he wants us to do, we look and long for something solid to cling to. According to 2 Timothy 3:14-17, however, we can be certain about one thing: God has revealed his general will for our lives in the Bible.

We learn several things about the Bible here. First, Timothy could depend on the teaching of his grandmother Lois and mother, Eunice, because they relied on Scripture (2 Timothy 1:5; 3:14-15). As teachers, they were important, but both they and Timothy were subject to their textbook, God's Word. Second, with the adjective *God-breathed*, Paul is emphasizing that the Bible carries the full authority of its ultimate source, God. Third, because Scripture is God-breathed, it's useful to us in various ways. It teaches what is true, refutes what is false, corrects us when we sin, and shows us how to be righteous.

Finally, God gave us the Bible to enable us to do good. We should consult the Bible whenever we want to learn more about God's good will for our lives.

We can discuss God's will on at least two levels. (1) We can talk about God's specific leading in each Christian's life. God uses each Christian's unique circumstances, personality, and spiritual gifts to accomplish exactly what he wants in that person's life. (2) God has a general will that every Christian is to follow. This lesson will help all of us realize that we can rely on God's Word to understand God's general will for all Christians.

Bible Exploration and Application

Give each person several 3x5 cards and a pencil, and say, "On each card, write one question you have about God's will for your life. The question may be general—possibly about your career. Or it can be specific—perhaps about how to respond to someone who has hurt you.

Where Do I Begin?

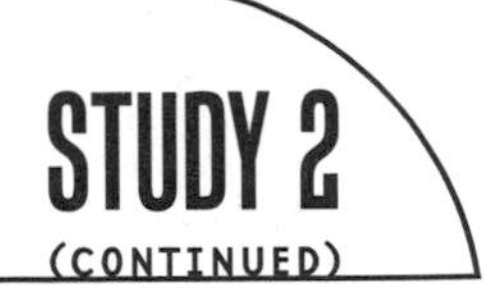

Write as many questions as you want. You won't have to reveal any questions you want to keep private, and I'll supply additional cards if you run out."

While people are writing, hang several sheets of newsprint where everyone can see them. After several minutes, ask for volunteers to share some of the questions they've written. Record their questions on the newsprint, leaving space to write under each question. For best results, list eight to 10 questions.

Have participants form groups of four. Direct each group to read 2 Timothy 3:14-17 and then discuss the following questions:

- What words does Paul use to describe Scripture?
- What does this imply about the Bible's relation to God? to God's will?
- In what ways does the Bible guide us toward God's will for our lives?

Have the smaller groups briefly report back their answers, and then say, "According to 2 Timothy 3:16-17, as God's Word, the Bible reveals God's general will for all Christians. Therefore, the Bible should be able to help us answer the questions we've listed."

Give each group a sheet of paper. Assign two of the questions on the newsprint to each group. (It's OK if several groups discuss the same question.) Tell group members to brainstorm biblical answers for each question. Groups can state general biblical principles or list verses relevant to the question. Either way, groups should state a biblical teaching and explain how it helps answer the question.

After 10 minutes, ask groups to report their insights to the whole group. Record the biblical guidance for each question on the newsprint. Then as a larger group, discuss the following questions:

- How easy was it to give biblical answers to your questions?
- How directly did the Bible answer your questions?
- What does this teach us about the Bible's role in helping us learn about God's will?
- How can we use the Bible more effectively in our search for God's will?

Say, "There's no better source of information about God and his will than the Bible. Because the Bible reveals God's general will for all Christians, we should begin our search for God's will with what God has revealed in his Word. And as we become more aware of God's general will in the Bible, we'll become more attuned to God's specific leading in our lives as well."

Closing

Put people back in their groups of four, and give each person another blank 3x5 card. Say, "We've talked about various ways we can follow God's general will for our lives, but now it's time to put our words into action. Take a moment to think of one way you'd like to follow God's will during the coming week. Now write what you've decided on your 3x5 card. After everyone in your group has finished writing, share with each other what you've written. To remind you to pray for the other members of your group, list their names and how they've decided to follow God's will on your card, and take it home."

Allow groups several minutes to write and share, and then have group members pray for each other, asking God for the wisdom and strength to keep their commitments to follow God's will.

After groups have finished praying, say, "The best way to begin following God is by following his general will as it's revealed in the Bible. Take your card home as a reminder of your commitment to follow God's general will and to pray that your group members do the same."

Who Am I, Really? STUDY 3

Read Ephesians 2:1-10. Then read the background information to see how the passage relates to people today. You'll need several pages of newsprint, several 3x5 cards, and pencils for this lesson (at least one of each of these for every member of your group).

Background Information

In Ephesians 2:1-10, Paul explains that God has made us alive in Christ. Sometimes thinking about who we *were* helps us see who we *are* more clearly. That's the approach Paul takes in the first three verses of this passage. He reminds us that we were once spiritually dead. Enslaved to sin and ruled by Satan, we went wherever and did whatever our hearts desired. Like everyone else without Christ, we lived under God's wrath.

However, that was before Christ. Now we have the basis for entirely new identities in Christ. First, we know that God loves us. God loved us even when we were ruled by sin and death. He loved us, not because of anything we did but because we are valuable to him. Knowing this should promote a healthy view of our own worth.

God has also made us alive with Christ. God didn't leave Jesus in the grave, and he didn't leave us dead in our sins. With our new lives in Christ, we can experience the abundant life that God wants every person to enjoy (John 10:10). We don't have to serve sin or fear death, for we are free to truly live.

In addition, we reign in heaven with Christ. When God raised Christ to heaven, he took us with him. We still live on this earth, to be sure, but our lives are in heaven with Christ. We're no longer under Satan's dominion. In fact, since we are in heaven with Christ, we are above this world and Satan, its ruler.

Finally, God has enabled us to do good. While our feeling of self-worth derives from God's love for us, our sense of purpose stems from the task God has given us. God wants us to perform good deeds that honor him. Our lives aren't pointless or of little consequence. Because of who we are in Christ, we can make a difference in the world and in the lives of others.

It's important to learn how inaccurate self-images affect the way we think, act, and relate to others, but it's not enough. We also need to see ourselves as God sees us. We need to understand who we are in Christ. Use this lesson to help the people in your group shape their views of themselves according to their true identities in Christ.

Bible Exploration and Application

Give each person a page of newsprint and a pencil. Tell members of your group to draw floor plans of their dream homes on the newsprint. Encourage them to use their imaginations and include anything that would make them happy, no matter how unusual it might seem.

When everyone has completed a floor plan, form groups of four. Direct group members to describe their dream homes to each other. Then have group members discuss the following questions in their groups. Ask volunteers to share insights from their discussions with the rest of the group.

- How do you feel about your dream-home ideas?
- What does the design of your dream home reveal about who you are?
- How is your design of a dream home like God's design of you?

Say, "The way we design our homes tells a lot about the way we live. In the same way, we can learn a great deal about who we really are by examining how God has designed us."

Have group members read Ephesians 2:1-10. While they're reading, write the following questions on newsprint, and put the pages up in front of the group. Tell the groups of four to answer the questions on the basis of Ephesians 2:1-10 and to be prepared to share their answers with the rest of the group.

- What are the characteristics of those in Christ? How are they different from those who are not in Christ?
- How does it make you feel to know how much God loves you? How should this influence the way we view ourselves?
- How does it make you feel to realize that God has not only made you alive but also made you Christ's representative on earth?

Ask for volunteers to share their groups' insights with the rest of the group. Then say, "Because of God's love for us in Christ, we're no longer bound by the sins and pains of the past. We're free to experience and enjoy the life that God designed for each of us. Because God designed us, he knows us better than anyone else, including ourselves. Let's take a few moments to ask God what his design for you is. Silently answer the following questions, and ask God's Spirit to help you see yourself as God designed you."

- What special abilities, gifts, or character strengths has God given you?
- What experiences has God used to help you grow?

Who Am I, Really?

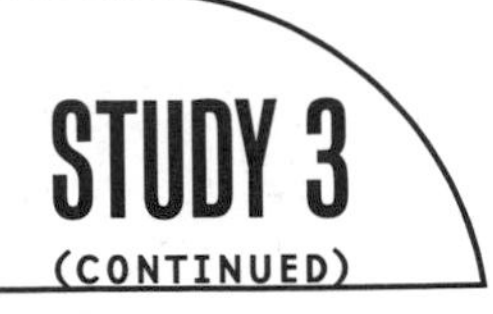

- What do you think God likes the most about you?
- In what areas do you think God would most like to see improvement?

After this time of reflection, say, "God loves us unconditionally, wants us to live contentedly, and trusts us completely to represent him. Since our true identities are found only in Christ, we need to set aside all of the inaccurate blueprints we have of ourselves and build our lives according to God's perfect design."

Closing

Keep group members in their groups of four. Give each person a 3x5 card and a pencil, and ask group members to keep the cards available in front of them.

Say, "One by one, pray for each person in your group, asking God to raise up that person's true identity in Christ in his or her heart. After you pray for each individual, write a descriptive name fitting that person's true identity on his or her card. For example, several people here might be named 'compassion' or 'mercy.' Choose a name that fits each person's special identity in Christ."

Dismiss groups after they finish praying. Encourage group members to keep their "name tags" as reminders of their true identities in Christ.

STUDY 4 What Do I Believe About Myself?

Read 1 Samuel 9:22–10:1; 10:19-24; 15. Then read the background information to see how the passage relates to people today. Have several sheets of newsprint available and enough thank you cards and pencils for each member of the group, as well as some additional writing material for your own use as study leader.

Background Information

In 1 Samuel 9:22–10:1; 10:19-24; 15, Saul gains and then loses a kingdom.

Saul had every reason to succeed. He was God's first choice to be Israel's first king. Moreover, he had been filled with God's Spirit and thus equipped to rule as God wanted (1 Samuel 10:9-11). Finally, since Saul was taller than every other Israelite, he even had the look and the stature of a king. In spite of all that, Saul failed miserably, a victim of his own insecurities and disobedience.

Part of Saul's problem may have been that he never expected to become king. One day he went looking for lost donkeys; he had no idea he would find a kingdom instead (1 Samuel 9:1-17). But when Samuel anointed Saul's head with oil, Saul should have known that he alone was God's chosen king. He also should have acted with the confidence that befits a king. Unfortunately, Saul shrank from his task from the very beginning.

First, Saul hid the fact that Samuel had anointed him king. Then, when Samuel tried to present Saul to the Israelites, God had to tell Samuel where to find the new king—hiding among the baggage; Israel's leader was too shy to appear before his people.

During the years that followed, it became apparent that Saul was also too afraid to lead the people. The clearest example of Saul's fear is described in 1 Samuel 15. God, through his prophet Samuel, commanded Saul to punish the Amalekites for their earlier hostilities against Israel. Saul was to completely destroy the Amalekites and their possessions. For the most part, Saul obeyed. However, he and the people spared Agag, the Amalekite king, and the best of the livestock (1 Samuel 15:9, 15).

When Samuel confronted Saul for his partial obedience, Saul first explained that the livestock had been saved to sacrifice to the Lord. Then Saul claimed that he had done everything God had ordered but that the people had disobeyed God (1 Samuel 15:20-21). Samuel wasn't convinced. He knew that Saul was at fault. He also recognized that Saul had never seen himself as God saw him, as king. Eventually Saul agreed: He had sinned because he was afraid of the people (1 Samuel 15:24).

Like Saul, many people today fail to live up to their potential because they see themselves

What Do I Believe About Myself?

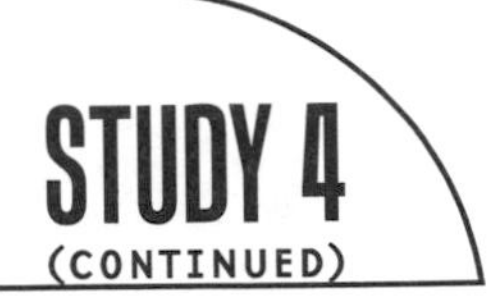

as inadequate. They're afraid that God will ask more of them than they can possibly deliver. However, we need to understand that God always enables us to become the people he wants us to be. In many cases, we simply need to see ourselves as God sees us.

Bible Exploration and Application

Have members of your group search the room for objects that represent fears they have about work, home, the future, their relationships, or some other aspect of their personal lives. They can each gather as many items as they want, but each person should find at least one item.

If the room you're meeting in doesn't contain much, bring some small items from home for the group to use in this activity. Your group can also use objects from their pockets, wallets, or purses.

After everyone has gathered at least one item, have the group members explain their items and the fears they represent. As each group member talks, keep a list of the fears mentioned on your own paper so you can discuss them later.

After everyone has shared, say, "Some of our fears are natural and healthy. For example, it's perfectly normal to be afraid when we stand near the edge of a cliff. Fear is an emotion designed to keep us out of dangerous or life-threatening situations. But sometimes fear is unhealthy. Sometimes our fears are based on false beliefs we have about ourselves. Let's examine how fear destroyed Israel's first king, Saul."

Have participants form groups of four, and assign half the groups 1 Samuel 9:22–10:1 and 10:19-24. Assign the other half of the groups all of 1 Samuel 15. Instruct groups to read their passages and then discuss the following questions. (To help groups remember the questions, write them on a sheet of newsprint, and hang it in a prominent place.)

- What fears does Saul appear to have?
- What faulty beliefs might have produced these fears?
- To what extent were Saul's fears justified?
- How did Saul's fears affect his behavior?
- What could Saul have done to overcome his fears?

Allow time for discussion, and then have participants form new groups of four, with two people who studied each biblical passage. Have group members report their discoveries to one another.

Then say, "It's pretty obvious that Saul was afraid to act like a king because he didn't

think of himself as a king. Unfortunately, the same thing happens with people today. For example, someone who's always afraid of losing her job may have a false belief about her own competence. Likewise, someone who's always afraid his wife is cheating on him may have a false belief about his own self-worth."

Read the list of fears people mentioned at the beginning of this activity, but without indicating who said what. Then instruct the groups of four to discuss the following questions:

- How are the fears we discussed earlier like Saul's fears? How are they different?
- What beliefs do these fears point to?
- To what extent are these beliefs false? To what extent are they true?

Give each person paper and a pencil. Have group members create three columns on their papers. Then have them list in the columns: (1) the fears their objects represent, (2) any false beliefs those fears might be connected to, and (3) what steps they can take to change those false beliefs. For example, someone might write for each column: (1) I'm afraid no one likes me. (2) My value is based on what I do, not who I am. (3) Memorize verses about God's unconditional love for me.

When everyone has finished writing, say, "The lies we believe about ourselves can control our lives. But half the battle in overcoming false beliefs about ourselves is simply recognizing what the lies are. Take your paper home, and use it as a reminder to battle the lies you believe about yourself with the truth of who you are as a special child of God."

Closing

Have participants form a circle, and distribute blank thank you cards and pencils. Read Philippians 4:8-9.

Say, "As God's children, we need to fill our minds with things that are true, noble, right, pure, lovely, and admirable. That includes the things we think about ourselves. Take a moment to silently ask God to show you one thing about yourself that is true, one thing that is noble, one thing that is right, one thing that is pure, one thing that is lovely, and one thing that is admirable. Write a thank you prayer to God for each of these things, and ask God to help you continue seeking the truth about yourself until you fully discover who you are in Christ."

Encourage group members to keep the cards in their Bibles and to refer to them often as they seek to uncover their true identities in Christ.

How Do I Choose What's Best? STUDY 5

Read Luke 10:38-42. Then read the background information to see how the passage relates to people today.

Background Information

Luke 10:38-42 relates a domestic conflict between two sisters. Martha is busy on behalf of others, preparing her home and a meal for the traveling teacher and his followers. Mary sits quietly at Jesus' feet, listening to what he's saying. As Martha serves Jesus and others, she seems to be fulfilling the two great commands. But when she's overwhelmed by the work and asks Jesus to tell Mary to help, Jesus commends the sister serving her own needs, not the one engaged in selfless service. The basis for Jesus' commendation of Mary (which appears to contradict his teaching in Mark 12:28-34) is explained by means of three contrasts.

First, Luke contrasts the postures of the two women. Mary sits at Jesus' feet in the position of a pupil or disciple. Martha, however, is initially "pulled away" by the distractions and comes to and stands beside Jesus only when she wants his help with her sister.

Second, Jesus contrasts the "many things" that distract Martha with the "one thing" that is needed or lacking. Serving others is commendable, but excessive service can create internal anxiety and external agitation. It can also pull our attention away from more important things such as listening to Jesus (Luke 10:39; see also 8:11-15, 21; 11:28).

Finally, Jesus presents an implicit contrast between Martha's good choice and Mary's better choice. Jesus never condemns Martha. He simply reminds her of the difference between our temporary needs (food) and our eternal need (knowing him). Mary had chosen something better, and Jesus refused to take this away from her.

Jesus said our two greatest responsibilities are to love God and to love others. But sometimes these priorities place conflicting demands on our time. Sometimes we must choose between the good and the better Let's look at how we can balance our primary need to know and love God with the important demands that loving others places on our time and attention.

Bible Exploration and Application

Before your group gathers, make a copy of "Don't Christians Cook?" on page 118 for each person in your group.

STUDY 5 How Do I Choose What's Best?

(CONTINUED)

Ask for four volunteers to present Luke 10:38-42. Assign them to play the roles of Martha, Mary, Jesus, and a narrator, and make sure each of them has a Bible to read their roles. Have Mary, Martha, and Jesus act out the parts as they read the words of their characters. (Mary has no speaking part.) Position the narrator to the side, and instruct him or her to read everything except the dialogue.

After the presentation, ask all those who think they're most like Mary to move to one side of the room and those who think they're most like Martha to move to the other side. Say, "Discuss the following questions in your group. Before you discuss each question, appoint a group member who'll report your ideas to the larger group later."

Ask the following questions, pausing after each couplet of questions (one each for the Marthas and Marys) to allow time for discussion and reporting:

- Marthas: How are you like Martha? What are the strengths of being like Martha? What are the weaknesses?
- Marys: How are you like Mary? What are the strengths of being like Mary? What are the weaknesses?

- Marthas: When have you been in a situation similar to that of Martha? How did you feel?
- Marys: When have you been in a situation similar to that of Mary? How did you feel?

- Marthas: What are some of the "many things" that worry you? Why do you focus on them instead of on more important things?
- Marys: What would happen if everyone sat at Jesus' feet? Why do you prefer sitting at Jesus' feet to being busy with work?

Then ask both the Marthas and Marys:

- What one question would you like the other group to answer?

Give groups time to come up with questions, and then have them take turns questioning and responding to each other.

Say, "The church probably wouldn't be a very healthy and happy place if everyone were like Mary in this passage all the time, or if everyone were like Martha. So we need to learn how God wants us to balance the two. To do that, let's study Luke 10:38-42 a little more carefully."

Form groups of three, with at least one Mary and one Martha per group. Give a copy of "Don't Christians Cook?" to each person. Tell people to answer the questions at the top of the handout and share their answers with the group.

When the groups have finished, ask for volunteers to report any insights they gained from the passage. Then instruct people to complete the bottom section of the handout.

When the groups have finished, say, "Sometimes our physical responsibilities conflict with our spiritual priorities; at other times various physical and emotional demands compete for our attention. However, at all times, God wants us to make time for the most important things. As we set time aside for what's truly important, we'll discover that the secondary concerns find their proper place in our lives and our schedules."

Closing

Say, "God wants us to make time for the most important things. We know that loving him is the most important thing, so let's make time now to express our love to him in prayer."

Form a circle. Ask people to each name one important thing in their lives that they're thankful for, and then invite them to contribute a spoken prayer of praise for those important things. Close by praying, "God, thank you for the important things you've given us. Help us make time for all of them. In Jesus' name, amen."

Encourage everyone to take a moment sometime during the rest of the day to thank God for the important things in his or her life.

Don't Christians Cook?

1. Read Luke 10:38-42. Discuss the first five questions in your group.

- What were the "many things" that made Martha anxious and agitated?
- What is the "one thing"?
- Do you think the "one thing" is the same in every situation? To what extent does it vary?
- What does Jesus' description of Mary's choice as "better" imply about Martha's choice?
- What does this passage teach about balancing our spiritual priorities and our physical responsibilities?

2. Write your answers to the following questions on this page. Then share your answers with the other members of your group.

- Currently, what are your two biggest spiritual priorities? physical responsibilities?
- How well do you balance these priorities and responsibilities?
- What secondary concerns distract you from your priorities and responsibilities?
- How can you eliminate or reduce some of these secondary concerns?
- What one thing will you do this week to make time for what's important?

Which Right Thing Is the *Right* Thing?

STUDY 6

Read 1 Corinthians 10:23–11:1. Then read the background information to see how the passage relates to people today. You'll need several pages of newsprint, dominoes, and several 3x5 cards and pencils for this lesson (at least one of each of these for every member of your group).

Background Information

God helps us determine what we should do in a given situation by offering us general values and principles to live by. In 1 Corinthians 10:23–11:1, Paul states two of those guiding values and then applies them to the Corinthians' situation.

The question for the Christians at Corinth was whether it was better to eat meat offered to idols or to avoid it entirely. Compelling reasons existed for either choice. While eating the meat could demonstrate someone's belief that idols are nothing and that everything belongs to God, onlookers might equate eating meat offered to idols with accepting idol worship.

Paul's answer to the Corinthian quandary is a model of wisdom and balance. Paul urged the Corinthians to take whatever action would bring God the most glory and others the most good. Sometimes, eating would glorify God and be a benefit to others. At other times, declining to eat would bring God more honor and others more good. Although any action was permissible for the Corinthians, all actions were not equally profitable and suitable for the situation.

Now, as then, blindly following one course of action in every situation can be dishonoring to God and harmful to others. It can also lead to an unbalanced and unhealthy life. Therefore, we need to identify how we can accomplish the greatest good and then do what's best in each situation. As we learn to do what's best at all times, we'll be able to maintain the balanced lives that God intends for us to enjoy.

Today we're going to focus on how to maintain balance in our lives by doing what's important and needed every moment of every day.

Bible Exploration and Application

Before class, use a marker to write each of the following phrases on a separate sheet of newsprint. Then hang each page in a different area of the room. Place a marker by each sheet of newsprint.

Which Right Thing Is the *Right* Thing?

- Time with God
- Time for family
- Time for Christian fellowship
- Time to serve others
- Time to get my work done
- Time for personal refreshment

Say, "God wants us to maintain balance in our lives. But most of us are stronger in some areas than in others. Read the signs posted around the room. Find one area that you're good at making time for, and stand by that sign."

After everyone chooses a sign, say, "For the next few minutes, you'll be working with the people who chose the same sign you did. If you're the only person at your sign, choose another area of strength. If five or more people are by the same sign, divide into at least two smaller groups."

When all the groups are formed, give each person an index card and a pencil. Instruct groups to discuss the benefits of making time for their areas and the consequences of neglecting those areas.

Allow several minutes for discussion, and then ask for a volunteer from each group to summarize the group's insights. After every group has reported, say, "Now that we understand why each of these areas is important, let's give each other ideas on how to make time for each of these areas. Have each member of your group share one idea that has helped him or her make time for the area you've chosen. One person in your group can write the ideas neatly on the newsprint."

After giving groups time to complete this activity, say, "Although God wants us to maintain balance in our lives, most of us tend to neglect at least one of the areas listed on the newsprint. Now find the area where you most want or need to spend more time, and stand by that sign."

As before, adjust groups so each has at least two but no more than four people. Have each group read and discuss the previous group's ideas for making time for that area. Encourage people to list on their index cards at least two ideas that they can personally implement during the coming week.

After five minutes, have groups read 1 Corinthians 10:23–11:1. Then direct group members to discuss the following questions:

- How will implementing your ideas help you better honor God? serve others?

Which Right Thing Is the *Right* Thing?

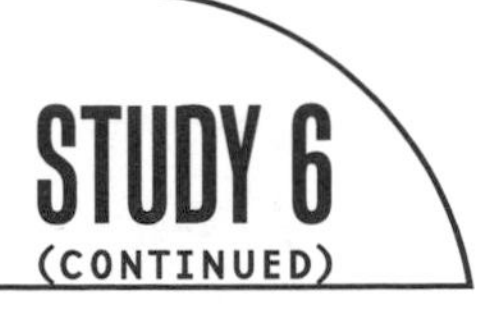

- What will be your greatest challenges to putting these ideas into action?
- What will be the benefits of implementing your ideas? What are the consequences of neglecting them?

Say, "Remember, God wants us to maintain balance in our lives, but it's our responsibility to make it happen. As you put your ideas into action during the coming weeks, you'll discover not only that you will honor God better and serve others more effectively but also that your life will become more balanced than ever before."

Closing

Gather the group around a table. Give each person a domino. Say, "Let's work together to build a well-balanced structure." Have group members incorporate their dominoes into a single structure, repairing and rebuilding it as necessary until it is sturdy and well-balanced.

Say, "God wants us to maintain balance in our lives. One way we can become better balanced is by supporting one another and encouraging one another to make time for every area of need in our lives."

Have people each find one other person from their second groups. Ask everyone to commit to putting into action one idea for maintaining better balance during the coming week. Encourage partners to agree to a specific plan of encouragement and accountability during the week. For example, partners might agree to meet for lunch, to pray for each other every day, or to talk on the phone at least once. Have partners pray for each other's specific needs for better balance. Then dismiss the group in prayer, thanking God for the freedom to give ourselves to a variety of activities and asking him to help each person maintain a well-balanced life.

STUDY 7 How Does God Guide Me?

Read Colossians 1:9-14. Then read the background information to see how the passage relates to people today. You'll need several pages of newsprint, extra paper, and pencils for this lesson (at least one of each of these for every member of your group).

Background Information

In Colossians 1:9-14, Paul informs the Colossian Christians that he regularly prays for them.

Paul had never visited the Christians at Colosse, but he knew of their faith in Christ as well as their spiritual struggles. So Paul prayed for the Colossians constantly, asking God to fill them with the knowledge of his will. The way Paul discusses God's will reveals several truths that anyone seeking to follow God needs to keep in mind.

First, Paul states that God gives us knowledge of his will through (or along with) wisdom and spiritual understanding. This implies that there's no inherent conflict between true wisdom and God's leading. At times, God's will may appear foolish to us, but it is always the wisest course we can take. In addition, Paul's reference to spiritual understanding suggests that the Holy Spirit is the one who gives us insight into God's leading. We might employ a variety of means in our search for God's will, but we're ultimately dependent on the leading of the Holy Spirit.

Paul also identifies the purpose of knowing, and the results of following, God's will. We should seek God's will so we're better able to live in a manner worthy of and pleasing to Christ. In other words, seeking to follow God means seeking to please Christ instead of ourselves.

Finally, following God's will produces at least four results in our lives. We "bear fruit," revealing God more to others through our own lives; we grow in our personal knowledge of God, become stronger in our ability to endure and be patient; and we learn to habitually thank God the Father for everything he has done for us.

The pursuit of God's will never ends during our time on earth. We're constantly discovering new aspects of God's leading in our lives and constantly encountering new situations in which we need God's leading. Let's explore how we can pursue God's will more effectively by looking at the variety of means we can use to discover God's specific will for our lives.

How Does God Guide Me?

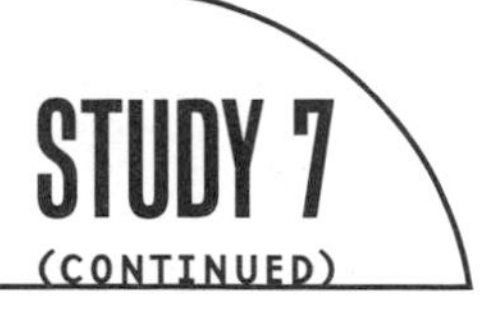

Bible Exploration and Application

Form groups of four. Tell each group member to describe one situation in which he or she had sought specific guidance from God. Encourage people to address the following questions as they describe their situations:

- How did you search for God's will in this situation? How well did your method of searching direct you to God's will?
- What would you do differently if you faced a similar situation today?

After everyone has described a situation, have group members discuss the following questions:

- In what ways were our situations alike? How were they different?
- How were our methods of searching for God's will similar? How were they different?
- What does the diversity of methods imply about discovering God's will?

Say, "It's encouraging to realize that we can discover God's specific will in a variety of ways. Still, as we seek God's will in each situation we face, we need to keep in mind what Paul teaches in Colossians 1:9-14."

Instruct groups to read Colossians 1:9-14. While groups are reading, write the following questions on a sheet of newsprint, and hang them where everyone can see them, leaving room under each question.

- What's the purpose of discovering God's will?
- What will be the results of following God's will?
- In what ways can we search for God's specific will for our lives?
- What things keep us from discovering God's will?
- How can we know whether or not we're following God's will?

Allow groups time to discuss the questions, and then ask them to report their answers to the larger group. Record their answers under the corresponding questions on the newsprint.

After every question has been answered, give each person a sheet of paper and a pencil. Have everyone answer the following questions on the paper. Allow time after each question for people to think about and write their answers.

- What's one situation you're facing right now in which you'd like God's leading?
- How have you sought God's will in this situation?

- What do you think God may want you to do? Why do you believe that this may be God's will?
- How can you seek God's further leading in this situation?

Say, "God is eager to lead us into a deeper knowledge of himself and his will. Because God reveals his specific will for our lives in various ways, we need to commit ourselves to look for God's leading in whatever way we can and to follow God's leading whenever we discover it."

Closing

Keep people in their groups of four. Say, "If we're serious about discovering God's specific will for our lives, we need to be willing to talk honestly and listen carefully. Let's close today's lesson by putting those skills into practice. First, let's talk and listen to each other."

Ask group members to share from their cards where they are searching for God's will. As each person names a situation, have the other group members offer encouragement or advice relevant to the situation. Encourage everyone to speak honestly and listen carefully for God's leading in the matter.

After everyone has shared, say, "It's helpful to talk honestly with and listen carefully to other Christians, but it's vital to do the same with God. So let's conclude our time by talking honestly to God and listening carefully to what he might say to us."

Have each person pray silently, asking God for guidance in the situation described earlier. Then have people reflect silently on how God might be leading in their situations. Some group members might want to read Scripture, while others might prefer to listen quietly for the Holy Spirit's leading. Encourage everyone to seek God in the way most comfortable to him or her.

After several minutes, close in prayer. Pray, "God, we want to thank you for providing a variety of means through which we can discover your will. Help us seek your leading in every situation we face. In Jesus' name, amen."

How Can God Best Use Me? STUDY 8

Read Ephesians 4:7-16. Then read the background information to see how the passage relates to people today.

Background Information

In Ephesians 4:7-16, Paul describes various gifts Christ has given to the church. This passage helps Christians see the value and the necessity of the different gifts God gives us. The role he has for each person—whether mentioned in this list or not—is crucial to the health and the ministry of the church. If the church is to serve God effectively, we must all do our parts.

Paul focuses on the importance of demonstrating our unity in Christ as we use our various gifts. Paul's picture of the entire "body" functioning through the mutual support of all its members depicts the ultimate goal for Christians in relationship with one another and with Christ. We're to work together to build up the church through the exercise of the gifts God has given us.

It's helpful to know that we have one overarching purpose in life: to serve God with all that we are as we seek to become more like Christ. This is God's will for us. God has given each Christian natural talents and at least one spiritual gift. Most Christians have also developed other skills.

God's will for our lives involves using all of these abilities to serve him in our unique circumstances and situations. Together, let's examine what God's will might be for each of us in serving him more fully.

Bible Exploration and Application

Have people form groups of three or four. Say, "Following God's will involves the way we put our faith into practice. Each of us has an important role in God's working in the world."

Have someone in each group read Ephesians 4:7-16 aloud. Have people discuss the following questions within their groups:

- What does this passage tell us about God's will for individual Christians?
- Which aspects of the gifts described in verses 11-13 have group members exhibited?
- How are each person's gifts valuable to the building up of the body of Christ?
- What other gifts and abilities can Christians put to use in the church today?

Ask for volunteers to report their groups' insights to the whole group.

Say, "God uses many different gifts and talents in the church, and God blesses his followers with unique abilities to carry on his work. God's will for our lives includes using our abilities and gifts to serve him. As we seek to discover God's will for our lives, we must consider how he wants us to use the skills and gifts he's given us."

Within their groups, have people take turns describing a gift or talent they've discovered and appreciated in another group member. For example, someone might say, "I'm excited to learn how much you reach out to children in your neighborhood" or "I've appreciated your leadership of our group today." Encourage people to express their appreciation as specifically as possible. As people share, go around to various groups and offer your own appreciation for the abilities you've discovered during class.

Closing

Before class, make one photocopy of "At the Crossroads" on page 127 for each person. Have people remain in their groups. Give a handout and a pencil to each person. Have people read and follow the instructions at the top of the handout.

After five minutes, ask people to share within their groups as many of their answers as they feel comfortable sharing. Have group members encourage each other and affirm each other's resolutions.

Then say, "God's will for our lives includes using our abilities and gifts to serve him. This handout helps us identify things we know God wants us to do as well as things we don't yet understand. As God continues to reveal his will to you during the coming months, refer to your handout and update your answers."

Have groups close in prayer. Begin by praying, "God, thank you for drawing us into relationship with you, and thank you for giving us unique and important tasks. Help me discover your will for me in the area of..." (Complete the sentence yourself, and invite members of your group to do the same.)

After everyone completes this prayer, have each smaller group form a circle. Instruct group members to take turns telling each other ways they believe God might use them in the future. For example, someone might say, "I think God might use your humor to help people see the brighter side of things." Encourage people to speak positively and sincerely about each other.

At the Crossroads

As you reflect on God's will for your life, fill in your thoughts in each section below. You won't be asked to share anything you'd prefer to keep private.

1. What things am I certain God wants me to do...
- regarding family issues?
- regarding my career?
- regarding the church?
- regarding my daily life?

2. What gifts and abilities has God given me?

3. Considering these gifts and abilities, what might God want me to do...
- regarding family issues?
- regarding my career?
- regarding the church?
- regarding my daily life?

Scripture Appendix

Verses Used in the Bible Studies

Study 1: Numbers 27:17; Psalms 95:7; 100:3; Ezekiel 34; John 9:13-34; 10:1-6, 24-30; 10:27

Study 2: 2 Timothy 1:5; 3:14-17

Study 3: John 10:10; Ephesians 2:1-10

Study 4: 1 Samuel 9:1-17; 9:22–10:1; 10:9-24; 15; Philippians 4:8-9

Study 5: Mark 12:28-34; Luke 8:11-15, 21; 10:38-42; 11:28

Study 6: 1 Corinthians 10:23–11:1

Study 7: Colossians 1:9-14

Study 8: Ephesians 4:7-16

Section Five: Media and Culture

As our worlds become more and more fragmented, the thing that tends to bind young adults together more than anything else is the unstoppable connection they have with the culture itself through a wide variety of media.

Music. It's so important to many young adults that they can't drive anywhere without first loading a favorite CD into the car's player.

News. Young adults make up part of the most important advertising demographic group. Someone is watching all those 24-hour news channels, and many of those viewers are young adults.

Movies. The social life of young adults often revolves around what new movies are being released each week, both on DVD and in theaters.

Reality shows. Not even young adults can explain this phenomenon. But ask your group—almost everyone has a favorite.

Internet. Not much to say, except that most young adults have never experienced life *without* it.

You get the idea. Media and culture are like a second language for young adults. The ideas in this section will help them be sure their faith remains vital amidst all the other influences that already saturate their lives.

In addition to the many ideas here, another great resource is Group's mediaandministry.com, which not only contains hundreds of reviews of movies, video games, music, and television shows, but also includes discussion starters that will help youth workers use all of the above media—as well as breaking news stories—to relate the gospel to young adults (complete with cautions as needed).

Truth in Plain Language

Read Acts 17:16-34 and the "to know" information in the following paragraph. Then, as a group, talk through the "to discuss" questions. Finally, help everyone remember the quick study by doing the activity in the "to do" section.

To know:

Throughout his ministry, the Apostle Paul made sure his words were appropriate to the people he was talking to. In this passage, Paul directed his message to non-Jews. Instead of explaining how Jesus fulfilled Old Testament prophecies—his standard approach with the Jews—Paul began his message by referring to a god the Athenians already worshipped.

For all their knowledge and wisdom, the Greeks were quite fearful when it came to religion. They worshipped many gods and were afraid to offend any other gods they might not know about. They even erected an altar "to an unknown god," seeking to cover all the bases and avoid the wrath of any god they might not be aware of.

Paul knew that the people really needed to discover the known God. Paul spoke to the Athenians on their own level, fully aware of their beliefs and clearly explaining God's working in terms they could understand.

In the same way, by telling people about Jesus in the plain language of today's culture, we can open the door to Christ for the people we work with, live with, or meet on the street. And we can trust the Holy Spirit to guide and help us as we do so.

To discuss:

- What did Paul refer to first as he began speaking to the leaders of Athens?
- What kind of language did Paul use in talking with them?
- What comforting thoughts did he give?

• Why do you think Paul quoted a Greek poet while preaching the gospel?

• What are some ways we can use Paul's approach in telling others about our faith?

To do:

Have participants form groups of four or five people, and have each group brainstorm a list of Christian jargon (words or phrases that have specifically Christian meanings). Instruct the groups to define the words and come up with alternative ways of saying them. The goal is to use the language of today's culture without weakening the meaning and truth behind the words. Ask the smaller groups to share the words and alternative words or phrases they came up with. Record the words and alternatives on blank newsprint; later, transcribe them and e-mail the list to everyone in your group.

Leader Tips

4 Leader Tips on Media, Culture, and Movie Nights

TIP 1

3 Great Reasons to Study the Culture

Young adults getting together to watch a movie or to have a discussion about something going on in the current culture isn't complicated, but it is worth adding to your young adult ministry. Here's why:

1. *You'll draw people who won't come to a "young adult ministry meeting."* Watching a popular video or TV show on DVD or discussing a secular book every two or three months is a fairly low-commitment introduction to building relationships with other young adults. Those attending aren't required to talk unless they want to, although most people will probably be comfortable enough to enter into discussion.

Think of culture-related events and activities as a threshold experience for young adults—a place where they can form relationships and start to build trust. It may be a steppingstone for more significant involvement in your ministry down the road.

2. *You can gauge people's spiritual condition.* Because discussions delve into significant topics already prevalent in the culture, the young adults who attend will reveal glimpses into what they think, feel, and value. Oddly, a group of young adults talking about renewal and redemption after watching *Groundhog Day* will probably say more than if they were sitting in a Sunday school class.

3. *Others will take ownership.* The same people who would never come to a "young adult ministry meeting" would never lead a meeting either. Yet they'll be excited about hosting a movie night or logging on to an interactive online activity.

TIP 2

Media Log

If some people in your group question how much the media and culture really influence them, try this quick exercise. Copy the form on page 134, distribute it, and have each group member complete it.

TIP 3

10 Tips for Leading a Young Adult Movie Night

Movie nights aren't just about watching movies. The point is to set up discussions and encourage fellowship among young adults. The movies are simply shared experiences and discussion prompts. Here are 10 principles for ensuring that the movies and the environment you select are appropriate:

1. *Meet in a home.* It keeps the cost minimal—just a video rental and snacks. And when people come into each other's homes, they form a natural bond.

2. *Don't announce the movie's title.* Some people might decide not to attend because they've already seen the film. But remember, the movie itself isn't the point. Discussion and fellowship matter more, so reveal the title when plates are full and people are already parked in front of the screen.

3. *Stick with PG or PG-13.* While there will always be something in a movie that might offend one person in your group, a PG rating usually ensures that the offense will be fairly minor.

4. *Serve movie food.* Popcorn, chips, pizza, candy, and soda will do it. Health nuts can eat better the next day. Ask each group member to bring something to pass around. This ensures that you won't go broke, plus it builds ownership of the event.

5. *Don't meet too often.* Maybe your group will want to get together every month or two. That frequency will still allow you to maintain the relationships you're trying to build, especially if your group does other activities together.

6. *Choose movies wisely.* While the host can decide what video or DVD to rent, members of your group agree that movies need to fit the following criteria: PG-13 or tamer, less than two and a half hours long, thought-provoking, and includes substantial spiritual and/or emotional content.

Media Log

Think back to yesterday. How much time did you spend reading, watching, or listening to various types of entertainment or news media? Take a guess, and fill in the time on the blanks below.

Music and Radio: ______________________________

____

TV/Movies: ______________________________

____

Internet: ______________________________

____

Newspapers/Magazines: ______________________________

____

Books: ______________________________

____

Video Games: ______________________________

____

Other: ______________________________

TOTAL: ______________________________

Now answer these questions:

- What was your total?

____

- What do you see as good or bad about the variety of media you use on a given day and the amount of time spent using it?

____

____

- How do you think the amount of media you consumed yesterday compares with the amount of time you spent with God yesterday (in prayer, reading Scripture, and so forth)?

____

____

7. No pausing. Once the movie starts, it keeps rolling. That means people need to plan ahead for bathroom breaks and refilling sodas. Why? If you stop any time someone needs to visit the little boys' or girls' room, you'll still be watching at breakfast the next day!

8. The host controls the remote. This is a matter of respect and resolves a battle before it ever starts.

9. The host starts the discussion. After the movie ends, it's part of the host's job to get the conversation rolling. The discussion may suddenly take a dramatic turn once it starts, but the first nudge is up to the host.

10. Keep this one to yourself. A question that *always* works when the discussion is floundering is "Which character in this movie do you most closely identify with, and why?" Tuck that question into the back of your mind, and pull it out if the discussion ever screeches to a halt.

TIP 4

8 Tips for Leading a Book Discussion

Encourage the book lovers in your group by having a regular book discussion night. The books you discuss don't have to be explicitly Christian in nature. Many secular novels also dig deeply into spiritual issues and may be an easier "in" for some of the young adults in your group.

Schedule your discussions for every month or two to allow everyone time to make it through the whole book. Here are eight principles for ensuring that your book discussion nights go smoothly:

1. Choose books that will challenge your group. Try to select books that have some degree of complexity or that raise tough issues. Books with multidimensional characters who have some hard choices to make are far more likely to inspire discussion than those with simple characters that are more plot-driven.

2. Come prepared. As group facilitator, make sure you show up with six to eight open-ended questions. Yes-or-no questions will stop the discussion in its tracks. Remind your group that there are not necessarily any right or wrong answers to your questions.

3. Have your group members come prepared as well. Ask each member of the group to come up with one discussion question of his or her own. Since everyone will focus on different parts of the book, everyone will gain new insights about both the book and each other.

4. Allow your group members to criticize a book, but don't let it stop there. Some great book discussions can result from discussing even those books that many people in your group disliked. Ask your group members: What didn't you like about the book? The style? The characters? The writer's worldview? Get them to share what they're thinking and feeling. At the same time...

5. Try to keep a balance between personal reactions and reactions to the book itself. Every reader's response to a book will be tied to his or her own experiences and worldview, but basing a discussion entirely around one's own thoughts and feelings can alienate others in the group who disagree. In short, make sure your book discussion continues to discuss *the book.*

6. Don't feel obligated to defend the book or the author. Your job is to facilitate the discussion—to give all group members a chance to be heard, whether you agree with them or not. Likewise, when someone makes an outrageous statement, don't feel you have to confront him or her. Kick it back out to the group: "Does everyone agree with Fred's comment?"

7. Keep the discussion moving. If one group member begins dominating the discussion, wait for his or her next breath and redirect his or her comments back outward to the group: "Let's focus on what you just said. What does everyone else think?"

8. Be a good listener. By doing this, you'll be able to fill in the gaps between each person's points. Make sure you hear what people are saying and think about how to restate their comments if there is an appropriate opening. Also, watch the facial expressions of your group—they'll often provide clues as to when people want to say something or when they agree or disagree.

20 Media and Culture Ideas

IDEA 1

Newspaper Watch

One great way to keep up with the culture and media is through the newspaper. Have your group do a weekly newspaper watch. You might want to start a weekly Bible study with this discussion. Collect articles throughout the week from national, international, and local papers. Some larger newspapers offer free registration to view content on their Web sites. Encourage the members of your group to browse through different papers and different features, giving emphasis to articles that represent worldviews that are new or foreign. (A worldview is an opinion or attitude concerning how the world works and why.)

To begin your meeting, have someone read highlights of a relevant current news article. Next, summarize what seems to be the main idea of the article. Then ask the following questions for group discussion:

- How does this article affect you personally?
- How does the article affect the church both in America and worldwide?
- What worldview do you feel the author is conveying?
- Is the particular worldview one the church can support? Why or why not?
- Where do you think the line should be drawn when it comes to Christians taking public stands on public or "private" issues, or do you think a line should be drawn at all?
- How can the church speak prophetically to the cultural issues covered in the article?

Close your time in prayer, asking God what voice the church should have on the issues you've discussed.

IDEA 2

Jesus in the Media

It is always interesting—and sometimes frustrating—to observe the ways Christ and the church are portrayed in the media. From debates over topics where the law of the land and the teachings of the Bible may or may not come into conflict, to controversial books or films being criticized by the church, to movies and television specials investigating or retelling certain biblical stories (often having little relation to the original biblical accounts themselves), God and his will are being discussed throughout the world, whether Christians are part of the dialogue or not.

Either as a homework assignment or, better yet, during your regular group night, watch an upcoming movie or "news special" in which God or the church is a central topic of discussion. Afterward, and depending on the type of show you watch, discuss the following questions:

- How did you feel watching this story? Did it make you reconsider any ideas you previously had on the subject?
- Do you think the facts were represented accurately in this story? Why or why not?
- Do you think God or Christianity was represented accurately? Why or why not? And if not, was it more the fault of the media or the people involved in the story?
- If a discussion about this story comes up when we go to work or school or have time with our friends tomorrow, what topics do you think will be brought up? What would your response be to those topics?

IDEA 3

Dream Couples

The magazine racks in your local grocery store and many of our television shows are saturated with images of the latest engagements—or divorces—of well-known couples in the entertainment world. Regardless of your feelings about these couples, their actions, or how they're portrayed, their experiences can serve as lessons for the rest of us.

Bring in a recent magazine article about one of these couples, or bring in more than one if you like in order to compare and contrast. As you talk about these couples, there will be an obvious temptation for the discussion to descend into gossip. Be careful to avoid this. Stick to the facts, as best as they're known, and remember that you're here to learn from their actions (and mistakes). Here are some questions that can be asked:

- How do you feel about this relationship? Do you think it's genuine? Do you think it has a chance of "going the distance"? Explain.
- How careful has this couple been in seeking privacy about their relationship? How important do you think privacy *is* to a relationship?
- How long should people date before getting married?
- How do you view dating? Is it fun? Is it dead serious? Is it somewhere in between? Explain.
- Would you ever date someone you wouldn't consider marrying? Why or why not?
- Is your faith more important to you than a potential marriage partner? Why or why not?
- Do you think religious differences are important when you're dating? Explain. How would you deal with those differences?
- Do you care what other people think about your dating choices? Do you listen to friends and loved ones who warn you about a potentially poor choice? Explain.

IDEA 4
You Are What You Read...?

Cultural expectations and ideals can affect and distort our relationships with the opposite sex. Encourage young adults to think more deeply about this with a discussion based on media images in popular magazines.

Ask your group members to bring in examples of magazines they've come across that portray certain perspectives and preconceptions about young men and women. (As group leader, use your judgment concerning which magazines are relevant and acceptable to the discussion.) Separate young adults into gender groups. Ask each group to glance through the magazines and discuss the roles and expectations in the pages. Here are some discussion questions to consider:

- What images of your gender are portrayed in these magazines? in the ads? in the articles?
- What do these magazines expect you to be interested in?

• What misperceptions are there? What truths?

• Compare the ads to the editorial content of the magazine. What effect do you think the photos in the ads are meant to have? Do you notice a difference in tone between the ads and the articles? If so, what is it?

• How does looking through the magazine make you feel about yourself? your life?

• What perception would someone of the opposite sex have of your gender after reading one of these magazines?

Allow plenty of time for this discussion. Finally, bring both groups together, and ask them to share their insights. Especially encourage each to elaborate on misrepresentations they observed and discuss what effects media like these have on male-female relationships.

IDEA 5

Messy Spirituality

In *Messy Spirituality,* author Michael Yaconelli challenges the notion that we must be perfect to be good Christians or to be spiritual. He lays out a spirituality for the rest of us—those of us who don't pray as much as we think we should, who are suffering through trials in life, or who simply feel like we don't measure up. His message is that God cares most about our desire for him, not whether we specifically pray for a half hour each day or can recite the Bible by heart.

Meet for eight weeks to discuss each of the eight short chapters of *Messy Spirituality.* If your group is large, divide into smaller groups for discussion times. Start each session with a brief synopsis of the chapter for any participants who weren't able to read that week. Then have participants discuss the chapter in their groups. Here are some specific suggestions for creative exercises to accompany the discussions each week:

Week 1: Provide finger paints, and ask participants to paint self-portraits depicting their messiness. Ask them to prayerfully consider whether the messiness they perceive is "messy" in God's eyes or just in the eyes of the world.

Week 2: Discuss the preconceptions surrounding the word *spirituality,* and then have participants write their own definitions of the word or draw pictures to show what spirituality looks like in their lives or the lives around them.

Week 3: Ask group members to read over the quotes from Nelson Mandela, Mark Twain, and Parker Palmer that begin the chapter. Discuss which quote they like best and why. Challenge each group to come up with its own statement reflecting the focus of this chapter.

Week 4: Hand out legal-sized sheets of paper to each participant, along with colored pencils and/or markers. Instruct group members to draw timelines of their lives. To get their thinking started, ask them to consider times God has broken through the everyday fabric of their lives—whether at a low point or a high point—and draw a vertical line to mark each of these moments. After participants have reflected and drawn their timelines, encourage them to share within their groups as they feel comfortable.

Week 5: Ask individuals to list all the ways they feel "odd"—different from those around them or not quite in line with the mainstream. Then ask them to consider which of their "oddities" are actually gifts from God and how they can use these oddities to express God's love.

Week 6: Instruct the discussion groups to discuss Yaconelli's four "nonprinciples" of spiritual growth, and challenge each group to come up with at least one additional or replacement nonprinciple. Have a spokesperson from each group share the nonprinciple with the whole group.

Week 7: Ask participants to write their own stories of "little graces," making sure they know that these stories will be read by others in the group. Compile the stories, with the names of each participant listed, into an "Amazing Graces" book. At the final meeting, present each individual with a copy of the book.

Week 8: Brainstorm ideas for sharing and spreading "God's annoying love" to the world around you.

IDEA 6
The Messages

Encourage young adults to look at popular biblical stories in a new way by comparing contemporary retellings and translations and writing their own. Choose a well-known story from Scripture, such as the parable of the prodigal son, the story of the woman at the well, Samson and Delilah, the crossing of the Red Sea, or another. Find the passage from a standard translation such as the New International Version or the New King James Version, as well as from more creative interpretations such as Eugene Peterson's *The Message* and Walter Wangerin Jr.'s *The Book of God.*

Have participants form groups of two or three. Have each group compare the various translations and interpretations of these well-known Scripture passages and then discuss the following questions:

- What were the different goals of each writer/translator?
- What details does each version seem to emphasize or minimize?
- What version do you prefer, and why?

Have each group sketch out its own contemporary retelling of the same story. This can be either a modern-day parallel in the news or in a movie or book, or a fictionalized retelling.

Bring groups back together. Ask a representative from each smaller group to share the retelling. Discuss these questions as a group:

- What did reading the different versions reveal about this familiar story?
- How can retellings of the biblical story help us better understand God's people and the way he works in our lives?
- Conversely, how can we make sure that taking literary liberties with Scripture doesn't cause us to misunderstand?
- In biblical times stories were mostly passed on orally. How do we pass on stories in today's world?
- Why are biblical stories so enduring in the fabric of today's secular world?

IDEA 7

Saint Julian

Commemorate the Lenten season and its themes of atonement and redemption with a discussion of the powerful novel *Saint Julian* by Walter Wangerin Jr. Allow group members a month or so to read the book.

If possible, schedule your meeting for Holy Week. Kick off the group's discussion with the following questions:

- What do you think of the narrator, the minor cleric? Why do you think the author chose him to tell the story of Julian?
- What biblical parallels do you notice throughout the book?
- The author gives no names to characters, except for Julian. What do you think of this? (See also the narrator's explanation at the end of Chapter 3.) How would the story be different if all the characters had names?
- What role do Julian's parents play in his story? How do they prepare him for the life they plan for him? for the life he ends up living?

• Early on, we see that Julian struggles with a dual nature—the intelligent, reverent future lord he presents to the world and his violent inner self. How did you react to Julian's acts of violence as they gradually grew in scale? Do you relate to this duality of self? Explain.

• What does it mean that the most shaming night of Julian's life is followed by his being awarded his greatest honor? How do you think Julian felt that day?

• Did Julian make the right decision by leaving his home? Explain.

• The Red Knight kills many, yet the one Moorish shepherd he kills is the one that comes back to haunt him. Why?

• What's your opinion of Julian's wife? Why does her love "torment" Julian? Was Julian right to leave her? Explain.

• The drama of Julian's fall, the depths he plunges to, can compare only to his spectacular redemption. What does the grotesqueness of the leper Julian ferries represent? What does Julian's redemption teach us?

• Which character in the story do you relate to most?

IDEA 8

Hit the Books

Use secular fiction novels to discuss essential spiritual issues with young adults. Schedule your discussion of the books for every month or two in order to allow both avid readers and more casual readers time to make it through the whole book.

Consider these suggestions for books, or choose your own:

• *Saturday* by Ian McEwen. This novel presents a day in the life of a neurosurgeon and could lead to an exploration of that elusive goal: happiness.

• *The Da Vinci Code* by Dan Brown. This controversial thriller purports that Christianity is a farce created by power-hungry political leaders.

• *Gilead* by Marilynne Robinson. This novel about an Iowa preacher explores issues of faith, family, and friendship.

As participants read the book for an upcoming discussion, they should take notes about spiritual scenarios and lines in the text. Most great novels include at least one of these classic themes: sin and redemption, suffering, the quest for meaning in life, guilt and the past, romantic love, sexuality, coming of age/identity development, death, family dysfunction, the existence of God, overcoming tragic circumstances, or the search for happiness.

The leader of the discussion can focus on one or more of these themes in the book and develop open-ended questions that will generate meaningful discussion and open the door for talking about how a Christian perspective compares or contrasts with what's presented in the book.

When the book club meeting finally arrives, consider gathering in a neutral location such as a local coffee shop or bookstore. Welcome everyone, and launch into the discussion. As you facilitate the discussion, be discerning and sensitive to the needs of any non-Christian participants. Often, this means not allowing the group to "over-spiritualize" things, yet also making sure the Christians in the group are free to express their views.

IDEA 9
Artist Gathering

Christian artists and supporters can sometimes feel lost in a local church scene that doesn't appreciate a broad spectrum of art. Help art-minded Christian young adults connect to those who think similarly.

Start by choosing a location that is aesthetically pleasing, such as a church decorated with stained glass, an old chapel, or a room in an older university. If none of the above is available, work with the lighting and décor in a room to add to the aesthetical appeal.

Invite Christians who are artists of all types to an artists' night out. Include musicians, poets, painters, and anyone else who desires to use his or her art and gifting for the Lord. Put up fliers in coffee shops, church bulletin boards, and art galleries to attract local artists looking for ways to glorify God with their art. Choose a theme that runs through the evening, and ask each artist to contribute. For example, if the theme is "God's Gracious Love," artists would depict this theme through their media. Various artists and art supporters from within your group could also be in charge of one practical aspect of the evening: Culinary artists could prepare hors d'oeuvres, musicians could supply the music, and so on.

The purpose isn't to glorify anyone's artistry but to celebrate a gifting that sometimes gets overlooked by the church. Ultimately, God bestows these gifts, and this evening will give artists an opportunity to give God the glory.

Finally, invite those who are not artists to enjoy the evening. Host a forum or discussion on art and faith with artists who feel comfortable participating. This could be a question-and-answer time with the artists, discussing their works and how they fulfill the event's theme as well as the artists' personal walks with the Lord.

IDEA 10
Art Walk

Find a location in your community that displays art, such as an art museum or a group of smaller galleries. Or drive to a nearby community, making a full day of this activity. If tracking down displayed art is impractical because of location, local libraries or bookstores will carry art books or your group can view art sites online.

Walk through the displays and "soak up" as much of the art as possible. Take mental notes or write down some thoughts about each piece of art.

- What do you like about the piece? dislike?
- How does the artist speak to you? Describe how the work makes you feel.
- What spiritual elements or themes do you perceive in the piece?
- What picture of the world is the artist describing?
- Is there room for God or Christianity in the piece? Explain.

Afterward, gather the group to talk about what you observed. Compare notes. Additionally, discuss the church's place in the art world and vice versa.

- Does it seem that churches appreciate art? Why or why not?
- How has the church's attitude toward art changed over time?
- What can the church do better to connect with the art world?

IDEA 11
Bringing Art Back Into the Church

Gather your artists—or just your young adults who enjoy drawing and doodling—for an evening to display their talents and glorify God, while creating works that can be appreciated by the entire congregation.

Ask your group members to bring whatever mediums they wish to use—pencil, watercolor, oil paints, whatever—to your next meeting. Once they're gathered, dig as a group into Jesus' journey to the cross. Ask individuals to read the following passages from the gospel of Matthew: 26:17-30; 26:31-35; 26:36-46; 26:47-56; 26:57-68; 26:69-75; 27:1-10; 27:11-26; 27:27-31; and 27:32-50.

When they've finished reading, ask your artists to select one of the above passages and create a work representing that piece of Scripture. For example, Matthew 26:36-46 could be anything from a full-scale drawing of Jesus in the garden to a picture of hands praying. What's important is that they convey the meaning of the passage, not necessarily their degree of artistic ability.

When the works are completed, bring the group back together. Ask your artists to explain their works and what their pieces of Jesus' sacrifice mean to them personally. Close with a time of prayer, thanking Jesus for all he has done for each person in your group. Make sure the works are displayed prominently in your church so others in your congregation can also appreciate what Jesus has done for them.

IDEA 12

The Simpsons

Find a copy of a season of *The Simpsons,* the long-running animated TV show about a dysfunctional but lovable family that interacts with neighbors, co-workers, and other members of the fictional town of Springfield. Get together in someone's home, and watch a few episodes (or more, if everyone is willing!) together as a group.

Afterward, talk about the spiritual themes that weave through the show—including family life, selfishness, faith, and friendship. Use these questions to get your discussion going:

- What scene was most significant to you? Why? What did you learn or feel?
- Which of the characters—Marge, Homer, Lisa, Bart, or others—do you relate the most to? the least? Explain.
- Where did you see characters showing Christ-like qualities or values?
- In what ways does this show inspire you to interact with your family? neighbors? family? God?

IDEA 13

Jerry's Nihilism vs. Jesus' Purpose

Rent some episodes of the TV classic *Seinfeld* on DVD, get together to watch them in one of your group members' homes, and then use them to discuss a Christian worldview. In the midst of the humor and laughs, the main characters in *Seinfeld*—Jerry, Elaine, Kramer, and George—are a portrait of a nihilistic worldview. Nihilism could simply be defined as an attitude that existence is senseless and useless. It's a view of life in which there is no solid basis for truth or morality.

In nearly every episode of *Seinfeld,* you'll find examples of nihilism in practice: the friends attempting to determine if an action is right or wrong simply based on their own consensus; a laissez-faire attitude toward the hardships or trials of others; a refusal to assign significance or meaning to core human issues such as religious expression, sexual union, or death; and countless other typical *Seinfeld* moments.

Show an episode or two with these thoughts in mind, but keep the tone of the evening lighthearted and fun. After watching *Seinfeld,* use these questions to stimulate discussion:

- What were the funniest parts of this episode?
- Who is your favorite *Seinfeld* character? Why?
- Which parts of this episode best relate to your everyday life or experiences you've had? Explain.

Then launch into a discussion of nihilism, making sure the group understands what the word means. Ask these questions to continue your discussion:

- Do you agree that the characters in *Seinfeld* generally hold a nihilistic view of life? Why or why not?
- What scenes or lines in this episode represent a nihilistic worldview?
- Based on your own everyday lives and the worldviews of your non-Christian friends, what are some other common examples of nihilism in action?

If you want to add a scriptural element to the discussion, ask participants to read John 10:10-11; Romans 8:28; Philippians 2:12-13; 3:12-14. Then ask the following questions:

- How do these passages contrast with a nihilistic worldview?
- From a Christian perspective, what is the meaning and purpose of existence?

• What are the practical implications of the belief that life is infused with purpose and meaning?

• How can we reach out to friends who have a nihilistic perspective on life?

IDEA 14
Hurt, and Trust

The late Johnny Cash's cover of the Nine Inch Nails' song "Hurt" is considered by many to be one of the most affecting songs (and music videos) in recent memory. In the video, scenes from the singer's life are interspersed with current shots of a fragile, 71-year-old Cash; as such, the video becomes a moving portrait of a man who had experienced much loss in his life but who was still keenly aware of God's grace, in addition to the powerful anti-drug message of the original song.

The video is downloadable from any number of sites, but if this is a logistical problem, playing the song (from the album *American IV: The Man Comes Around*) will be effective enough. After playing the song or video for your group, discuss the following questions:

• What feelings do you have after watching the video (or listening to the song)?

• What do you think is the significance of Cash's late wife, June, watching over him as he sings? What emotions does each of them appear to be experiencing?

• The song's chorus declares, "You could have it all/My empire of dirt." When have your own hopes and plans become nothing more than an "empire of dirt"?

• Read Isaiah 40:1-8. What does this verse tells us about where our trust should be?

• What areas of your life have you not yet given over to God? How can you begin to hand those things over to him?

IDEA 15
Grace Makes Beauty

The song "Grace" from U2's album *All That You Can't Leave Behind* paints a unique and poetic picture of grace.

Start by listening to the song from the CD, and then use the following questions to spark the group's discussion:

- Define *grace*. What do you think the biblical use of the word is, and how is the word used differently by those outside the church?
- What do you think the words "[Grace] carries a pearl in perfect condition" mean?
- Another line in the song says, "What once was friction/What left a mark/ No longer stings." Do you think this is a good description of biblical grace? Why or why not?
- Read John 1:14. Can you think of examples in Jesus' life when he fulfilled this description?
- What acts of grace did he show to others even when they seemed undeserving of his grace?
- What grace does Jesus offer you even when you don't deserve his grace?

IDEA 16
A Cold and Broken Hallelujah

The Leonard Cohen song "Hallelujah," made popular by the movie *Shrek* (via the John Cale version in the movie and the Rufus Wainwright version on the soundtrack) and also covered by a number of other artists including Jeff Buckley and Bono, can spark discussion about several issues, including male and female relationships.

Find one of the above versions of the song, and play it for your group. Then divide participants into groups of three or four to discuss the lyrics and the following questions:

- What are the biblical references in the song?
- Does the fact that the song refers to biblical stories make this a Christian song?
- What makes a song Christian or secular? Is there always a clear distinction? Explain.
- "Hallelujah" is a love song of sorts. What is the overall theme of this song or its message about romantic relationships?
- Read Judges 16:1-22 and 2 Samuel 11:2-4. What is the message of these stories? How do they fit into the overall biblical picture of male-female relationships?
- What does the word *hallelujah* mean to you? What do you think about the way this sacred word is mixed with images of physical love?

• What do you think is meant by "a cold and broken hallelujah"? When have you uttered a cold and broken hallelujah?

Bring the smaller groups back together to share insights. Close by singing the praise song "Alleluia."

IDEA 17

There Will Be a Light

There Will Be a Light is a beautiful gospel offering from Ben Harper and the Blind Boys of Alabama. Listen to as many of the songs as the group wants to, or look at the song lyrics together by passing around the CD jacket.

The songs on this album focus on significant topics such as redemption, healing, church, love, family, forgiveness, and prayer.

To get a discussion going, use the following questions:

• How does this music affect you emotionally? Why?

• What view of God is represented here? How similar to or different from yours is it?

• What messages does this music have on truth? hope? Jesus? forgiveness? sin?

• How can we use this music as a way to come before God in prayer and worship?

IDEA 18

Take My Life

U2's song "Yahweh" (from *How to Dismantle an Atomic Bomb*) and Frances R. Havergal's hymn "Take My Life and Let It Be" follow a similar lyrical pattern: focusing specific aspects of everyday life and offering them up to God. "Yahweh" takes a somewhat repentant tone; the words represent a messed up, sinful Everyman who cries out to God to redeem the various aspects of his life. Havergal's hymn has more a feeling of devotion and commitment and is a more direct and purposeful proclamation of Christ's lordship in the life of the singer.

Invite participants to silently read the lyrics of "Take My Life and Let It Be," and then ask them to share with a partner specific ways they feel compelled to dedicate their lives to God. The following questions can help the discussion:

- How do you want to serve him more with your time?
- How do you want to more wholly dedicate your talents to God's purposes?
- How do you desire to worship him more with words and song?
- How do you want to use your hands and feet more directly for service to others?

After the discussion, dim the lights, and ask young adults to close their eyes and pray along with the words of a song. Play U2's "Yahweh." When the song ends, transition immediately into a time of spoken prayers. Encourage participants to tell God directly how they want to be fully committed to him.

IDEA 19

My Song

At the end of a meeting of your group, ask the young adults to each bring a song to your next gathering that they think best represents them. The song can be secular or sacred. It might be a song with lyrics that describe them, or it can reflect what they want to be. Or perhaps it is meaningful because of the year it was released.

At the following meeting, have individuals take turns sharing their unique songs. Break into groups of five to seven so everyone gets a turn.

Ask group members to each bring a song to the next meeting that reflects their spiritual lives and relationships with God. Share with each other in the same way.

Use these discussion-starter questions during both song activities:

- What does this song reveal about who you are?
- What do you feel and think when you hear this song? Why?
- In what ways are you unique, just as this song is unique?
- If you could change or highlight any of the lyrics of this song, what would you choose, and why?
- How can this song help you grow closer to God or know God better?

IDEA 20

Online Shoe-Shopping

Gather around a computer with an active Internet connection. Head to www.rejesus.co.uk/encounters/steps_faith/index.html.

Here you'll find an image of 20 pairs of shoes that represent 20 specific ideas for applying faith to life.

Say, "A critical part of our spiritual growth is taking steps of faith: refusing to stay the same and striving instead to take on challenges in order to become conformed to the image of Christ. Each of these pairs of shoes represents an action we can take as a response to God's grace and love in our lives."

Invite participants to sit at the computer one at a time and select a pair of shoes. (Everyone else should be gathered nearby to see what is happening onscreen.) When a participant moves the mouse over a shoe, he or she should read aloud the life-application challenge "tag" that appears.

After everyone has had a turn to read a "steps of faith" application suggestion, say, "I'd like us to take on one of these challenges this week. You can select to take the step of faith you clicked on, or if another one was more applicable to where you need to grow, do that one instead."

Give participants a minute to think about the steps of faith they'll take. Ask each person to find a partner, and encourage the pairs to share their steps of faith. Spend time praying in the pairs, asking God to help you put your faith into action.

This idea is just one of many devotional experiences you'll find at www.rejesus.co.uk. Rejesus is a British nonprofit Christian Web-based ministry, focused both on reaching out to spiritual seekers and to the spiritual formation of Christians. Check out these other rejesus pages with ideas you may want to try with your young adult group:

- www.rejesus.co.uk/encounters/quote_unquote/index.html—This page contains tons of quotes about Jesus, stretching back to the first century A.D. and up to the present day. Invite participants to surf through the quotes as a way to launch discussion about Jesus. For example, young adults could each select a quote that best represents their own view of Jesus, or they could find quotes that they think are most representative of society at large.
- www.rejesus.co.uk/spirituality/post_prayer/index.html—Group members can "light" a candle by clicking on it and posting a prayer. Participants can also read the other prayers and can pray for those requests.
- www.rejesus.co.uk/spirituality/labyrinth/index.html—This is an electronic journey through a Christ-focused online spiritual journey. Individuals should don the headphones for this 40-minute prayer exercise in which they'll contemplate their own spiritual journey and worship Christ as the focus of their existence.

20 Young Adult Movie Nights

For the bad reputation movies sometimes get in church circles, films can be pretty amazing. Movies at times can express spiritual issues and truths (or lies) in a more compelling way than a Bible study or sermon.

Still, it's important to realize that having a movie night with a group of young adults isn't the same as having a Bible study or discussing a sermon. Instead, the questions listed after each movie are meant to prompt young adults to explore the spiritual issues raised in the movie and to talk about their own lives and their own relationships with God.

Three suggestions about leading a movie night discussion:

1. Don't let anyone dominate the conversation. This can happen several ways, so look for these personality types at your young adult movie nights:

• The *therapist* is very comfortable with opening up (or expecting others to do so) in a group setting. This person may confuse a simple movie night with group therapy. This person will want to explore deep personal issues at length and share poignant stories that illustrate his or her inner conflict. Gently let therapists know that while conversation can—and should—dip beneath the surface, few people are ready to go too deep with emotional or spiritual topics.

• The *evangelist* is always looking for a way to bring the discussion back to the need for Christ. While this isn't a bad thing in itself, a faith decision isn't the point of every movie. Remind evangelists that movie nights are about forming relationships. It's these growing relationships that will give them permission to speak truth into each other's lives.

• The *jokester* isn't comfortable with getting personal, so he turns every comment into a punch line. Eventually, this shut downs conversation—who wants to share anything when there's a good chance you'll be harpooned with a joke? Gently challenge the jokester's behavior, even pulling him or her aside away from the movie night, if necessary. Don't be dissuaded by the distancing humor.

2. Ask follow-up and personalizing questions. If Jack says he thinks Mr. Holland (in *Mr. Holland's Opus*) sold out for a paycheck instead of starving until he became a famous composer, you might ask, "How important is it to do something significant?" If Jack says it's very important, gently probe further by personalizing the next question: "It sounds like several of us agree, but none of us have written a famous opera yet. How important is it to do something significant before we die? What might that be? What would it be for you?"

3. Set some ground rules. After a few movie nights, your group will develop a rhythm for discussions. But it never hurts to put a few ground rules in place and review them occasionally. Here are some you should consider:

- This is a group discussion. Make sure everyone has opportunity to comment.
- It's OK to disagree but not to be disagreeable. Every point of view will be respected.
- No double dipping in the salsa.

That pretty much covers it. Your group will probably be pretty much self-governing during discussion times after that. People may challenge each other's comments but not in a demeaning or critical way.

Actually, there *is* one more thing: Federal copyright laws do not allow you to use videos or DVDs (even ones you bought yourself) for any purpose other than home viewing. Therefore, if you have a large young adult group or are using a location larger than someone's living room (such as, for instance, the church sanctuary), it's best to cover yourself legally. Your church can obtain a license from Christian Video Licensing International for a small fee. Visit www.cvli.org or call 1-888-302-6020 for more information.

Napoleon Dynamite (2004) MOVIE 1

Genre: Comedy

Length: 86 minutes

Rating: PG for thematic elements and language

Plot: Napoleon Dynamite is a high school student struggling to define his identity in a world of bullies, geeks, family quirks, and social awkwardness. While managing his relationships with his brother and schoolmate Deb, he takes on the great challenge of helping his friend Pedro run for student body president.

Discussion Starter Questions:

- Why can the teenage years be some of the hardest we go through?
- What are the particular challenges to developing our own identities? Against what forces or people do we develop our identities?
- How do people learn to express themselves freely?
- What role does God play in the development of our identities?
- Study the story of Zacchaeus in Luke 19:1-10. How did Zacchaeus' identity change? What did Jesus do to bring about the change in his identity?
- How does Jesus free us to be ourselves?

MOVIE 2

Luther (2003)

Genre: Historical Drama

Length: 113 minutes

Rating: PG-13 for disturbing images of violence

Plot: The movie follows the life story of the controversial reformer Martin Luther. From his earliest days of teaching to his later days of leading a revolution, Luther's life is humorous, exciting, and risky. His movement spawned new denominations within the church and led to reforms of corrupt leadership. He took on all of his work passionately.

Discussion Starter Questions:

- Which of Luther's personality characteristics stand out most to you?
- Why do you think he was so passionate about knowing God?
- Why do you think he created such a controversy through his teachings?
- How does Luther inspire you?
- Look at 2 Timothy 3:16-17. How can the Scripture itself inspire us?
- What would it take to bring about revolutionary change in the modern church?

Finding Neverland (2004)

Genre: Drama

Length: 106 minutes

Rating: PG-13 for mild thematic elements and brief language

Plot: Playwright James M. Barrie watches as his most recent play receives a reception that is lukewarm at best—and truthfully, it didn't excite him either. Soon thereafter, while walking his dog Porthos through the park, he meets the four Llewelyn Davies boys and their widowed mother and is taken with them, especially Peter, who is still angry and emotionally distant over his father's recent death. Despite the objections of the boys' grandmother and his own wife, Barrie continues to meet with the boys and encourages them to use their imaginations. As he does so, his own imagination begins to unlock and new characters begin to emerge: a crocodile with the clock in its belly, a group of orphans called the Lost Boys, a fairy named Tinker Bell, and a boy named Peter Pan.

Discussion Starter Questions:

- How did Barrie's encouraging the Llewelyn Davies boys to use their imaginations help them deal with the tragedy in their lives? How did it hurt them?
- Were there times imagination was powerless to help the characters in this movie? What does this teach us about the limits of imagination?
- How much of Barrie's relationship with the Llewelyn Davieses was an example of "a childlike spirit," and how much of it was escapism? Give examples.
- What would you have said to Barrie concerning his growing emotional attachment to Sylvia?
- How did others view Barrie's actions and behaviors? What does this tell us about how people might see us when we get involved in others' lives?
- What does this movie teach us about the power of creativity and its ability to affect the lives around us?

MOVIE 4

Elf (2003)

Genre: Comedy/Family
Length: 95 minutes
Rating: PG for some mild rude humor and language
Plot: When oversized elf Buddy discovers that his true origins don't lie at the North Pole, he goes to New York to reunite with his real father. There he encounters what might be described as culture shock, as his cheerful holiday spirit is not well-accepted or understood. Still, Buddy sets out to restore hope and happiness to his family and the city.

Discussion Starter Questions:

- Where does Buddy get his personality? Where does he get his size?
- To what degree are our personalities shaped by our families?
- How might we develop value systems that are different from those of our families?
- How do we offer faith to our families?
- Read 1 Timothy 5:8. Why does Paul place such a high priority on caring for your immediate family?
- What challenges do we face in helping our families believe?

The Incredibles (2004)

Genre: Animated, comedy
Length: 115 minutes
Rating: PG for action violence
Plot: Mr. Incredible has hung up his superhero suit to take on the daily life of an insurance salesman, but something inside him misses the old days. His new call to superherodom involves his entire family in the plans of a diabolical, failed hero's attempt to gain the attention of the world.

Discussion Starter Questions:

- What gives the Incredibles their strengths and weaknesses as a family?
- Read 1 Corinthians 12:4-11. How are spiritual gifts like the Incredibles' gifts?
- How are Christians uniquely gifted to serve the world?
- Why don't spiritual gifts seem as exciting as superpowers? How can we make spiritual gifts an exciting part of our lives?
- What kinds of adventures might God be calling us to?

MOVIE 6

Hero (2002)

Genre: Action/Adventure, Foreign
Lengt h: 99 minutes
Rating: PG-13 for stylized martial arts violence and a scene of sensuality
Plot: An unknown warrior named Nameless delivers a message to the king: that he has vanquished the three assassins who had been trying to take the king's life—Broken Sword, Flying Snow, and Sky. He recounts how his fighting skills and cleverness brought the three enemies of the state down. However, the king perceives dishonesty in the story, and Nameless reveals his true reason for visiting the king.

Discussion Starter Questions:

- What moral values do you see being pitted against each other?
- Why do you think Nameless came to the conclusion that he did?
- Read Matthew 5:38-42. How is this value reflected in Nameless' conclusion?
- What sacrifices are people willing to make in the film?
- What are the "fights" that you're taking on in your life?
- What ways do you need to surrender your desire to control life?

Mystery Men (1999)

MOVIE 7

Genre: Action, Comedy

Length: 121 minutes

Rating: PG-13 for comic action violence and crude humor

Plot: Seven rather feeble superheroes band together to stop Casanova Frankenstein from his plans to take over the city. Using what are at best embarrassing superpowers, the team does what it can to compensate for its lack of gifts with teamwork.

Discussion Starter Questions:

- Why would people try to use meager gifts to make heroes out of themselves?
- Read Romans 12:4-8. How are spiritual gifts like and unlike the gifts of the Mystery Men?
- How do spiritual gifts work? How can you best use yours?
- What difference does it make when we use our gifts as a team rather than alone?
- How is the church like the Mystery Men?

MOVIE 8

Cast Away (2000)

Genre: Adventure, Drama
Length: 143 minutes
Rating: PG-13 for intense action sequences and some disturbing images
Plot: Chuck Noland is lost on a deserted island after a plane crash. He discovers that his life as a timely Federal Express worker quickly fades away, and he gradually learns the process of survival as his life transforms into that of a castaway. His discovery will never allow him to return to life as it was before.

Discussion Starter Questions:

- How do you think Noland's life will be after returning to civilization?
- Why do you think he goes the way he does in the end?
- If you had to live on a deserted island, what would you want with you?
- What would keep you hoping for the future?
- Read Hebrews 11:1. How is faith a source of hope?
- What promises does God offer us that keep us hopeful when we're alone?

Big Fish (2003)

MOVIE 9

Genre: Drama, Fantasy, Comedy

Length: 125 minutes

Rating: PG-13 for a fight scene, some images of nudity, and a suggestive reference

Plot: Big Fish is a fantasy drama that reads like a fairy tale. A web of unreal stories told from father to son creates a lifetime of strange memories. In the end, the son goes looking for the truth behind the tales to find the man his father really was.

Discussion Starter Questions:

- What made the son go looking for the truth behind the stories of his father's life?
- When do stories capture our attention? When do they become frustrating?
- Read John 1:10-14. What makes it hard for us to know our heavenly Father?
- What stories point us toward our Father, and what stories point us away?
- How do we become a part of God's story?

MOVIE 10 School of Rock (2003)

Genre: Comedy
Length: 108 minutes
Rating: PG-13 for some rude humor and drug references
Plot: Dewey Finn has no real career and no real future, even as the heavy metal guitarist he longs to be. However, when he answers a call intended for his roommate, he finds himself teaching at a local elementary school. With no real experience in teaching, lesson plans, or credentials, he decides the best he can do is put instruments in the students' hands and make them a band. Enrolling them in a local competition, he realizes that he cares more about the students than he had planned.

Discussion Starter Questions:

- How did Dewey find a cause to invest himself in?
- Are you more like Dewey at the beginning or Dewey at the end of the movie?
- What causes make your life worth living?
- Read Matthew 22:37-40. What are the purposes that Jesus says are worth living for?
- How are these purposes similar to the ones Dewey discovered? How are they different?
- How can those purposes give you the kind of enthusiasm that Dewey had by the end of the movie?
- What stands in our way of living for those purposes?

Ray (2004)

Genre: Biography, Drama

Length: 152 minutes

Rating: PG-13 for depiction of drug addiction, sexuality, and some thematic elements

Plot: The movie follows the biography of legendary musician Ray Charles. From a life of poverty and early blindness, Charles developed a stellar career, but one that came with the curses of infidelity and drug abuse. Yet his career would go on to revolutionize the music industry and engage the civil rights movement.

Discussion Starter Questions:

- What did Ray live for?
- How do you think God played into his life?
- What kept Ray from living for God?
- Read Exodus 20:1-6. What were Ray's idols?
- What things tempt you to make them into idols?
- What keeps your life from slipping away from God and into idolatry?

MOVIE 12

Mean Girls (2004)

Genre: Comedy
Length: 97 minutes
Rating: PG-13 for sexual content, language, and some teen partying
Plot: A typical day in high school reveals girls who maintain the social hierarchy by bullying each other. Cady Heron moves to the school and is taken under the wings of some of the worst of them. Drawing on her childhood experience in Africa, she studies the behavior of these new creatures—high school girls. Yet as much as she wants to be accepted by the rich and popular crowd, she finds that adopting their manipulative habits makes her dislike herself.

Discussion Starter Questions:

- How accurate do you think this portrayal of high school is?
- Were there times in high school you felt like you had to change your personality in order to fit in?
- What drives our need to fit in?
- Read Romans 12:1-2. What does Paul challenge us to do instead of conforming to the world around us?
- How do we achieve this?
- What makes it a challenge?

Envy (2004)

Genre: Comedy

Length: 99 minutes

Rating: PG-13 for language and sexual/crude humor

Plot: Nick Vanderpark makes a fortune on his new invention, leaving his neighbor and best friend, Tim Dingman, in the dust financially. Nick proves to be a generous friend who makes every attempt to include Tim in his new lifestyle. Still, Tim is overwhelmed with envy and can't stand to see his friend's success.

Discussion Starter Questions:

- How would you feel if your best friend suddenly became successful beyond your wildest dreams?
- How does money control the way we treat each other?
- Do you long for this kind of success for yourself?
- Read 1 Timothy 6:6-11. How have you seen this to be true?
- What can we do to monitor envy in our own lives?

Pirates of the Caribbean (2003)

Genre: Action/Adventure, Fantasy
Length: 143 minutes
Rating: PG-13 for action/adventure violence
Plot: Captain Jack Sparrow has lost a ship to a mutiny and is now looking for a new one. When he saves the governor's daughter, Elizabeth, from a near drowning, he is immediately thrown in jail because pirates can't be trusted. However, Elizabeth is kidnapped by Jack's old enemy from the mutiny, and Jack goes looking for her. Jack only lets on later that the mutinous pirates suffer a horrible curse: They are the living dead.

Discussion Starter Questions:

- Fate and fortune play a major role in the story of this movie. How does Jack see his fate?
- What decides Jack's future?
- Read Ephesians 1:3-10. How does the Bible describe our fate and future?
- How does it make you feel when your plans for life are suddenly changed without warning?
- How does this text from the Bible affect your view of change and surprises?

The Terminal (2004)

MOVIE 15

Genre: Comedy, Drama, Romance
Length: 128 minutes
Rating: PG-13 for brief language and drug references
Plot: Viktor Navorski finds himself trapped in a New York airport when his home country goes to war. He does not have proper credentials to leave the airport, and no plane will take him home. As a consequence, he learns to eat, sleep, and survive in the airport. Airport security personnel and other employees come to love him or hate him. Some try to push him out of the airport while others keep him going. At the same time, Viktor falls in love with a woman he meets in the airport, even arranging for a special dinner hosted by some of the airport staff.

Discussion Starter Questions:

- What about Viktor's personality helps him survive when he's trapped?
- When in life do you feel trapped?
- What kinds of forces or people trap you?
- Who sides with you when you're trapped? Who works against you?
- Read Galatians 5:1. How does Jesus make us free? From what?
- What virtues does Jesus build in our hearts that help us survive challenges?

MOVIE 16

Hotel Rwanda (2004)

Genre: Drama, War
Length: 121 minutes
Rating: PG-13 for violence, disturbing images, and brief strong language
Plot: The true-life story of the 1994 genocide of nearly a million members of the Tutsi tribe at the hands of the Hutu militia, and Paul Rusesabagina, who summoned extraordinary courage to save the lives of more than a thousand of the Tutsi refugees by granting them shelter in the hotel he manages.

Discussion Starter Questions:

- How did you feel after watching the movie?
- How could God allow something like this to happen?
- Discuss this statement made by Jack to Paul after he films part of the genocide on camera: "If people see this [video tape], they'll say 'Oh my God, that's horrible.' Then they'll go on eating their dinners."
- Discuss the poignant scenes of Tatiana (Paul's wife) and the cross she wears.
- Do you think Paul was a "Christ-like" character? Why or why not?

Groundhog Day (1993)

Genre: Comedy, Fantasy, Romance

Length: 101 minutes

Rating: PG for some thematic elements

Plot: Bitter, unkind newscaster Phil Connors is forced to live the same day over and over again. He experiences everything from anger to despair to hope as he experiments with many ways to live the same day. Eventually Phil finds redemption, joy, and love—and is transformed in the process.

Discussion Starter Questions:

- If this movie has a message, how would you sum it up in one phrase?
- Describe a time in your life you felt "stuck." What finally got you "un-stuck"?
- What actions might this movie compel us to take in our lives?
- In what ways do you relate—or not relate—to Phil?

MOVIE 18 The Village (2004)

Genre: Drama, Mystery, Thriller
Length: 108 minutes
Rating: PG-13 for a scene of violence and frightening situations
Plot: *The Village* appears to be set in the pioneer days, with a small puritanical town of families living in their own utopian community. All is well and happy in the village, with one exception: the deadly threat of creatures that live outside the town's borders. The village elders go to great lengths to keep the townspeople within their borders, constantly emphasizing the incredible danger of the creatures outside.

Discussion Starter Questions:

- Did the village elders have a noble goal in starting the village? Why or why not?
- In your opinion, where did they go wrong?
- What similarities do you see between the church's relationship to the "outside world" and the mind-set of the village leaders?
- What differences do you see between the village and the modern church? What's significant about those differences?
- What are the "creatures" in culture that the church avoids or protects itself from? Are these creatures a legitimate threat?

Leap of Faith (1992)

MOVIE 19

Genre: Comedy, Drama

Length: 108 minutes

Rating: PG-13 for language

Plot: A famous evangelist, Reverend Jonas Nightengale, comes to town with his tents, his miracles, and his profiteering. Little does he know that God sometimes works despite his messengers.

Discussion Starter Questions:

- Why do people follow charismatic leaders, even when they're frauds?
- What effect do preachers like Jonas have on our culture?
- How has God made surprise appearances in your life?
- Read Philippians 1:15-18. What do you think of the message of those verses in relation to this film?

MOVIE 20 The Lord of the Rings Trilogy

The Fellowship of the Ring, The Two Towers, The Return of the King (2001, 2002, 2003)

Wherein all the rules about keeping the movies under two-and-a-half hours are broken. Not to mention warnings about trilogies.

It's your call whether to do these as three separate movies or attempt an all-day or all-night marathon. If you *do* show these as three separate movies on separate occasions, bear in mind that you'll have to do some explaining of background and characters for those people who haven't seen the earlier parts of the trilogy.

Genre: Fantasy, Adventure, Action
Length: 178 minutes, 179 minutes, 201 minutes
Rating: PG-13 for epic battle sequences and scary images
Plot: These three movies center on a group of friends from various races and lifestyles (including hobbits, elves, men, and dwarves) who set forward on a life-threatening mission together against a common evil.

Discussion Starter Questions for *The Fellowship of the Ring:*

- Why does power tend to go to people's heads? What are some subtle, everyday ways our desire for power can express itself, even in doing "good" things?
- What ordinary people do extraordinary things in the movie?
- Read 1 Corinthians 1:25-31. Why do you think God so often uses the weak people or things of this world to do amazing things for his kingdom?
- How can you guard yourself from being corrupted by the desire for power?

The Lord of the Rings Trilogy MOVIE 20

Discussion Starter Questions for *The Two Towers:*

- How did the ring affect Frodo? Gollum? Faramir? Saruman? How do you think it would affect you?
- How is the One Ring similar to sin? How have you seen a sin or addictions transform and control someone? How does a person break free?
- What causes do you think are worth going to war over or dying for? What are some inappropriate causes that people have fought for? How does a person decide when to flee and when to fight?
- How does war affect the participants? those on the sidelines? Why is everyone affected by a war, whether they participate directly or not?
- When have you had the least amount of hope, and what happened? Did you rely on God during that dark time? Why or why not?
- How can a person learn to cling to hope at all times?

Discussion Starter Questions for *The Return of the King:*

- How did the ring corrupt Smeagol? How was his transformation into Gollum similar to what sin does to a person?
- Why are we so drawn to activities we know will eventually hurt us? How can you protect yourself from being tempted?
- How did Sam exhibit loyalty to Frodo? Do you think our society honors loyalty? Why or why not?
- Which characters showed leadership skills in the movie? Why did people follow them? How does following God naturally make a person a leader?
- Where did you see teamwork in the movie? Why is teamwork crucial for people who are trying to achieve the impossible?
- What "battles" do you see raging around you right now? What obstacles stand in the way of teamwork? How can we knock down these obstacles?

MOVIE 20 The Lord of the Rings Trilogy

General Discussion Starter Questions:

- Which character do you relate to most? Why?
- What would you choose as the most powerful scene? Explain.
- How and when do you see the following qualities represented: forgiveness, sacrifice, true friendship?
- How can you connect what the characters experience to our experience as Christians? What are similarities and differences?
- In what ways can these movies encourage you in your relationship with Jesus?

Section Six: Outreach

Outreach can be a scary word. It conjures up images of going door to door, trying to convince total strangers to pray to receive Christ. Of course, some people are gifted evangelists, and their ministry might involve doing just that. But most members of your young adult group will run screaming in the opposite direction if this is the goal of your outreach activities.

Instead, think of outreach as a very natural way to grow your group. For example, the members of your group invite friends who are already Christians but who don't have a church home to visit your meetings. Other times, group members will naturally reach out to non-Christian friends at school, work, or the gym and ask them to visit a special activity. Occasionally, you'll even create events at which they will meet total strangers and practice the beginning stages of evangelism.

But there's no reason to be afraid. By experiencing enough of these activities in your program, the members of your group will get better at "reaching out" by practicing. And the more they do this, the less afraid they'll be.

The ideas here will help group members get involved in inviting others—that's all outreach is. And the ideas will help those you touch see that your young adult ministry has something to offer: a welcoming, friendly, and loving group of people who love and follow Christ.

Quick Study

Actions Speak Louder Than Words

Read John 17 and the "to know" information in the following paragraph. Then, as a group, talk through the "to discuss" questions. Finally, help everyone remember the quick study by doing the activity in the "to do" section.

To know:

Jesus prays first for himself and next for his disciples. Then Jesus prays for future generations of followers, including us. Jesus asks that all who believe in him will be one, and he gives a model for the unity of Christians: the oneness of Jesus and the Father. A little later in his prayer, Jesus connects unity with the love talked about earlier: "May they be brought to complete unity to let the world know that you sent me and have loved them even as you have loved me" (John 17:23).

This passage concludes with Jesus' commitment to continue making his Father known to the world (John 17:26). How does he intend to do that? Largely through Christians' love for one another! But only through Christ's presence in our lives are we able to follow his command to love one another.

Here's something to think about: Jesus says the world will know that we are his followers by our love for one another. Conversely, could it be said that when we don't love one another, it's not very likely that the world will recognize us as Christians?

To discuss:

- If John wrote to our church today, what do you think he'd tell us we're doing right?
- What would he tell us about our unity and loving one another and how it compared to what he observed in Jesus?

• How can we show more unity and love within our church? within our group? within our community?
• When a family struggles to express its love, it's still a family. When a church struggles to express its love, do you think it's still the church? Explain.

To do:

Have everyone stand. Then say, "Let's put Jesus' command to love one another into action. When I say 'start now,' I want you to move about the room and talk to one another. First, you'll find a partner and tell each other how much you appreciate each other—and maybe even say, 'I love you.' After 30 seconds, I'll tell you to switch partners and start over, so make sure each of you gets a chance to say something within that 30 seconds. Let's take a few minutes to show our love through our words. Start now."

Every 30 seconds, signal members of your group to switch partners. When everyone has had a chance to talk to all the others in the room—or when you run out of time—have the group members form a circle and join hands. Pray that as your group desires to make an impact on the world around you, you'll be purposeful in your love for one another first.

3 Leader Tips on Outreach

TIP 1

7 Questions to Prepare Your Group for Outreach

As you plan how your young adult group will reach out, these questions can help you make sure group members are prepared.

1. Does our group truly want to reach out to others?
2. Are we committed to bringing new people into our ministry if our outreach activities are successful?
3. Have we evaluated the special talents and abilities of members of our group and tried to discern how God can use those?
4. Are we providing training so group members can best use their gifts in outreach activities?
5. Have we clearly targeted who we're trying to reach?
6. Have we made a list of the needs that exist around us so we can prioritize the most crucial needs and try to meet them?
7. Have we sought the involvement of all group members in deciding what outreach activities to undertake?

TIP 2

4 Basics for Young Adult Outreach

As your group gets ready to dive into outreach together, consider these basic "heart" principles for connecting with others.

1. Demonstrate your group's love and care. Learning how to be a caring group takes time. People love to be with friends, and they'll naturally seek out a warm, loving, and caring group. The best way to reach out is when satisfied people (your group members) tell others about the source of their satisfaction. A friend is the most influential means of bringing people to faith, reaching out through love and caring.

2. *Use outreach to practice what you're learning as a group.* Bible knowledge is important in your group, but knowledge without life application is of little value. As you lead your group, it's important to create ways for young adults to put into practice what they're learning. Focus on helping create spiritual maturity in the life of the group's members (Colossians 1:28). This is vital as you think of connecting with others outside your group because what we *believe* should determine how we *act* as Christians.

3. *Make outreach a priority for your group.* If you have no goals, you'll never know if you've reached them. Goals are simply what you reach for, something to help your group keep focus. Outreach needs to be a primary goal in your young adult group.

4. *Be creative and innovative with outreach opportunities.* In today's busy culture, you simply can't do business as usual. If you want your group to participate fully, outreach opportunities must be meaningful and practical.

TIP 3

Pray, Pray, PRAY!

Form a prayer team of volunteers who will commit to pray regularly for young adult ministry outreach efforts.

The prayer team can also take problems and questions to the Lord in prayer. When you're investigating whether your group should go in a new direction, ask the prayer team to petition God. Whether your decision is about what events to plan or what Bible study curriculum to use, ask God what he wants your group to do. Encourage the prayer team to ask God for direction, discernment, wisdom, and confirmation for the decisions you've made.

After the prayer team has brought your requests before God, patiently wait for his answers. Encourage those who are praying to write down verses or thoughts that come to them after their times of prayer. This allows all members of the group to share the prayer team's sense of the Holy Spirit's direction.

20 Outreach Ideas

IDEA 1
Swap Meet

Sponsor a swap meet that you can invite young adults to. Each person who attends should bring three gently used items that he or she already owns. Set parameters for what the items should be—for example, books, CDs, DVDs, or T-shirts. Advertise the swap meet at local bookstores, college campuses, and coffee shops, and encourage regular group members to invite friends, co-workers, and neighbors.

Before the swap meet, create fliers about other upcoming young adult activities. Before the event, set out drinks and crank up some lively praise music. Label a table for each type of item, and as people arrive, instruct them to set their items on the corresponding tables. You might need to do a little friendly quality control. If someone walks in with a paint-stained, ragged shirt to swap, you might suggest that they swap just two items instead of three. Of course, don't intentionally alienate anyone with too many rules.

Set aside a half hour for everyone to look over the merchandise. This is also a great time for regular members of your group to introduce themselves to new people. Have participants draw numbers to determine the order they'll choose swap items. Continue with the turns until each person has selected three items.

IDEA 2
Hot Topics

Schedule a monthly Hot Topics Night where group members can discuss controversial topics with theological implications such as celibacy, abortion, the supernatural, and capital punishment. In addition to the opportunity for outreach, this event will challenge those already in your group to think about their own positions and clarify what the Bible says about these controversial issues.

Announce each month's topic in advance so the members of your group can mention it when they invite others. Consider meeting away from church in a member's home or at a local coffee shop or bookstore.

Before each Hot Topics Night, prepare a worksheet that discussion groups can use. Include several open-ended questions and a list of relevant Bible verses. For help in coming up with topics and preparing the worksheets, refer to *20 Hot Potatoes Christians Are Afraid to Touch* by Tony Campolo (Thomas Nelson) and *Hot Topics, Tough Questions* by Bill Myers (Bethany House). For current topics, check out www.christianitytoday.com/ctmag/features/issues.

When young adults arrive for the discussion, form groups of four or five. Make sure to include at least one regular member of your group in each smaller group. Provide the worksheets, extra Bibles, and a timer or stopwatch. Each group should designate one person as the discussion facilitator, who will help ensure that each person gets to speak and decide when to move on to the next question. Each group should also designate one person as the timekeeper, who will start the timer when one person begins talking and let individuals know when time is up. This ensures that no one completely dominates the conversation.

The overall leader can walk around the room; listen to the various conversations; and remind groups to stay on topic, use their timers, and check out the Bible verses. Because these are "hot" topics, the leader will also try to prevent any discussion from getting *too* heated. Step in if you see a disagreement growing out of hand, and act as neutral facilitator, asking each person to outline his or her position without personal attack. You might need to recommend that they move on to the next question on the list.

As everyone grows more comfortable with the format, you may be able to let the discussions become less formal.

Call the smaller groups together 15 minutes before the scheduled end of the meeting to allow some time for visiting and/or cooling down. Thank participants for coming, and allow those who need to leave to do so. If any people want to engage in more discussion, invite them to form one group or talk with you at another time. Before anyone leaves, be sure to announce the time and topic of the next Hot Topics Night.

IDEA 3
Unfinished Projects

We all have at least one project that haunts us—that pile of photos we keep meaning to put into an album, that woodcarving project we never quite complete, or that piece of handmade paper we want to make into a unique birthday card for a friend. One night a month, schedule a Project Night for group members and visitors to bring their scrapbooking, woodworking, card-making, and other project supplies to church, spread them out on a long table, and work as they talk. People will also get tips and hints from others who attend.

Hold open hours such as 6 p.m. to 10 p.m. so people can come and go as they need to. Make sure at least two people already active in your young adult ministry are committed to staying the entire time.

Set up several long tables or large round tables, and cover them with butcher paper or vinyl cloths. Depending on the interests of your group, you might want to have tables marked for specific kinds of projects. Set out some general supplies such as scissors, craft glue, screwdrivers, and tape for everyone to use. Have snacks and drinks available, and be sure to provide child care so parents can participate.

Advertise your Project Night at local craft, scrapbooking, and home-repair stores and on local college campuses. Depending on the interests of your group, you can even schedule guest speakers to give short presentations—for example, a Home Depot or Lowe's employee to give tips on home projects or someone from a local scrapbooking store to demonstrate techniques and display sample pages and new products. The guest speakers can then stick around and offer advice and help.

IDEA 4
Full-Court Press

Everyone loves college basketball, right? Introduce new people to your young adult fellowship by sponsoring a March Madness competition. In March, when the teams have been selected, print out brackets for the college basketball tournament from espn.com or another sports Web site, and invite your church's young adults and their friends to fill out their predictions. Winners can receive prizes of gift certificates to a local bookstore or mall. Encourage regular members of your group to hand out the blank brackets at their offices and gyms. Limit each person to one entry, and collect all entries before the first game.

Calculate the winners by awarding one point for each win predicted in the first round, five points for wins in the second round, 10 points for wins in the Sweet Sixteen round, and so on.

Invite everyone who enters the contest to a viewing party of the Monday night championship game. When the winner is declared, finish your calculations and present the prizes to the winners of your contest. (You might want to specify that the winners must be present at the viewing party to collect their prizes.) It's also fun to give awards to second, third, and *last* place entries.

IDEA 5
Calling All Foodies

A great way to combine fellowship with outreach is to create a gourmet cooking group within your young adult group. A lot of young adults are learning how to cook—or, for the first time in life, they have the cooking tools and kitchen space to try a major culinary project.

Set a date for each month's dinner, and recruit one person or couple to host for that month. The hosts are responsible for creating the menu and selecting recipes from a cookbook or cooking web site. An easy way to do this is to focus on different types of food each month—for example, Italian, Chinese, Mexican, Greek. The hosts will provide beverages, prepare the main dish, and assign the rest of the recipes to the other members of the group. The others will cook the food according to the recipe and bring the prepared dish to the dinner to share. Depending on the size of your group, you can have either a seated formal dinner or a casual buffet-style meal. For larger groups, you can have several gourmet clubs going at once, each group preparing the same recipes.

Each regular group member should invite one additional person or couple—just be sure to RSVP to the host. Newcomers can eat the first time without bringing a dish, but to return, they'll have to cook, too. Have copies of all the recipes available at the meal for each person to take home if he or she wishes. You can set out a list of upcoming young adult activities and church contact information next to the recipes or even copy it on the back of the recipe pages.

IDEA 6

Singles' Bars

Invite young singles to a special study designed to meet their unique needs. To invite friends with no church affiliation, create special "invitations" to hand out.

Think of five or six people from your established young adult group to comprise a basic core for the singles study group. Ask them to help you create labels to put around chocolate bars. The labels should include all the information guests will need to attend your study, along with the verse "Taste and see that the Lord is good" (Psalm 34:8).

Challenge each person to distribute at least 10 of the "Singles' Bars" to friends outside your main group. You can also create small displays and leave chocolate bars in a campus student union, coffeehouse, popular restaurant—any place appealing to young adults. If cost is a concern, use snack-size bars.

This tasty invitation is sure to whet people's appetites. Host the meeting at a coffee or dessert shop so those attending can mingle and get acquainted in a casual setting. Use Psalm 34:8 as your theme for the first gathering.

IDEA 7

Exotic Locales

Stop trying to get new people to come to your Bible study. Instead, go to *them*!

Have a traveling group study that meets in different public places each week—high-traffic places where your group is sure to be noticed. Assign several people to be "greeters," on the lookout for anyone who seems interested in what's going on. Ask these greeters to introduce themselves and welcome newcomers to the group.

Brainstorm locations in advance, drawing on the insights of group members. List popular hangouts, and think of various scenarios to make these locations work. This might include the lounge area of a college dormitory, a trendy restaurant, or a cappuccino cafe.

Besides introducing yourself to people in the community, the variety will make the meetings fun for your regular attendees, as well as less threatening to those who may find it intimidating to walk through church doors.

IDEA 8

Unhappy Hour

Designate 3 p.m. on Sundays as "Unhappy Hour." During this time, challenge regular members of your ministry to actively seek out those who are hurting. They should use this time as an opportunity to reach out to other young adults in their circle of friends or in the greater community.

Let group members know that you'll spend the entire hour in prayer for them and the people they'll counsel. Equip them with encouraging Bible passages to share, such as Jeremiah 29:11-13; Romans 8:31-39; Hebrews 4:14-16; and 1 Peter 5:6-10.

In addition to their own friends who are struggling, your group can help at local agencies that serve the community, such as crisis pregnancy centers, nursing homes, and halfway houses. Don't overlook the obvious—a park bench, a restaurant, or the mall. Challenge your group to be more proactive in reaching out to anyone, stranger or friend, who is hurting.

IDEA 9

Mixed Drinks

For all those young adults who always dreamed of operating their own lemonade stand: Set up a free drinks booth at a college sporting event; on campus; or in the parking lot of a fitness center, movie theatre, or apartment complex within walking distance of a college campus. Be sure to get permission first.

Make this drink booth a standout by offering "mixed drinks." Buy dozens of cans of generic soda in off-the-wall flavors. Then invent your own names for special concoctions made up of combinations of the weird flavors—for example, create "Strawberry Shortcake" by adding one part strawberry soda to one part cream soda. Write the invented names on a piece of poster board (along with their secret ingredients) so people can place their orders and join in the fun.

Use this as an opportunity to invite young adults to your group. In advance, use a permanent marker to write Revelation 22:17 on the cups that drinks will be served in: "The Spirit and the bride say, 'Come!' And let him who hears say, 'Come!' Whoever is thirsty, let him come; and whoever wishes, let him take the free gift of the water of life."

When people ask you to explain the cryptic message, you'll have an easy opportunity to invite them to visit one of your regular group meetings or young adult Bible studies.

IDEA 10
The Perfect Man

Ask your group to help you compile a list of qualities that set Christ apart as the perfect man. Have T-shirts printed for group members to wear. Instruct the silk screeners to print "Let me introduce you to the perfect man" on the front of the shirt. On the back, include a drawing of Jesus and the descriptions your group has brainstormed, perhaps in a wild variety of fonts and sizes. Somewhere on the T-shirt, include the regular meeting times and location of your young adult group. T-shirt wearers serve as walking advertisements!

Challenge your group members to wear their T-shirts to the gym, on campus, shopping, and socializing. Prepare them to answer questions people might ask. If a question comes up that people can't answer, that opens the door to invite the questioner to visit your group.

IDEA 11
April 15th

Young people new to the workforce may have many questions about filing taxes or investing their newly earned cash. Create a Saturday when young adults from the community can meet with financial-savvy Christians who can answer their questions one on one.

Ask bankers, accountants, and other fiscally wise individuals from your church to volunteer a Saturday afternoon in March. If possible, advertise the event on radio stations and in the paper using Psalm 24:1 as your theme: "The earth is the Lord's, and everything in it, the world, and all who live in it."

Include this verse on banners, and photocopy it onto plain white paper for use as scratchpads. Also list your group's meeting time and location.

Set up tables in a large room at church with the volunteer money experts sitting on one side. Place an empty chair across from each person. Be sure individuals who come seeking advice also receive a special invitation to your young adult group study. Encourage the financial volunteers to write their notes and advice onto the scratchpaper so people take home a copy of the thought-provoking Scripture verse and the invitation to your group meetings and events.

IDEA 12

Living Mannequins

If any of your group members excel at the blank stare and lifeless demeanor week after week during young adult meetings, God even has a way for them to serve. Enlist their help as living mannequins to help advertise special outreach functions.

Position them at key locations such as the sidewalk near a busy intersection, a college dormitory, the parking lot of a discount store, or a student union (with the owner/manager's permission, of course). Supply signs and theme-related apparel, and use your live mannequins to invite passersby to your young adult events. For example, for a pizza party you have coming up, dress your still models in delivery-boy apparel, and tape signs to the front of pizza boxes to advertise the time and meeting place.

To draw a crowd and a lot of attention, your mannequins will need to stay completely still for a long period of time. This will generate plenty of interest, and it allows those in your group who sometimes feel they have little to offer the opportunity to reach out in a unique way.

IDEA 13

Cook Off

Advertise a cook-off contest that both regular attendees and visitors can get excited about. In this event, everyone prepares a secret recipe and brings it to your church fellowship hall. Provide a theme such as barbeque, soups, or international. Make sure each person prepares enough of his or her dish to serve 10 people, and give each person 10 tickets to distribute to young adults he or she wants to invite.

Place all the dishes on tables set up in a line, each one numbered. Place a voting box at the end with pencils and slips of paper. Then let in the masses! Have volunteers at the door to collect tickets, welcome newcomers, and instruct them on how to get started. Provide bowls and spoons, and let the guests sample the dishes. When they have finished, ask them to cast their vote for their favorite dish.

Be sure to offer fun prizes to the chefs at the end of the evening. Encourage those actively involved in your young adult ministry to mingle, introducing themselves to people they don't know and inviting them to your regular meetings.

IDEA 14

The Great Debate

Do some research online, and ask others you know in the ministry to refer you to a top-notch creation scientist. College campuses are a hotbed for extreme and often unchristian thought, leaving a lot of young adults confused about what to believe. This spills over to recent graduates and young adults new to the workforce.

Schedule an evening when the creation scientist can make an appearance. Advertise the event on campuses, at coffeehouses, in bookstores, and in other places young adults hang out. Be sure to extend the invitation to anyone you know who would like to ask questions of the scientist.

When young people discover that the Bible can intelligently respond to questions they may have about science and their origin, they may be more open to exploring Scripture with your young adult group.

IDEA 15

Love Fest

Because so many young adults are making decisions about the people they will spend the rest of their lives with, one very practical way to meet their needs is to invite young couples to a marriage preparation seminar that your group hosts. Plan for the event to last four hours on a Saturday or Sunday afternoon or evening. Ask three couples in your church who have happy marriages lasting 25 years or more to speak for up to half an hour each. Ask the couples to each share 10 tips that have made their marriages successful.

A pastor or counselor with experience in premarital counseling can also offer two half-hour sessions. The counselor should address the practical issues every young couple needs to think about—money, children, in-laws, sex, and dealing with conflict. Schedule 10-15 minute breaks between each session and a half-hour open forum at the end for couples to ask questions of your experts and discuss these topics with each other.

Members of your young adult ministry can provide theme-related snacks for the event, such as wedding reception–type cake and punch. Or keep things simple with snacks like a box of chocolates, heart-shaped sugar cookies, or conversation heart candies. Let those supplying the food be creative.

Be sure to have information on your young adult group's activities available in printed form, and be sure couples know that they're welcome to visit the group and your church at any time.

IDEA 16

Friends—Not Projects

Sometimes it can be easy for Christians to spend all their free time with other Christians. While this can be a great incubator for fellowship, it can also hinder our effectiveness in sharing Christ with those around us. If we don't have any relationships with non-Christians, how can we tell them about Jesus?

The first step is to encourage your group members to build authentic relationships with people already in their lives. The goal is not to see these people as projects but to develop real relationships.

First, help your group members think of unchurched people in their lives. These might be classmates, co-workers, neighbors, or members of clubs they belong to.

Next, if necessary, help them narrow down their lists to two or three people who they'd genuinely like to build deeper friendships with but just haven't had the time or initiative to do so.

Finally, spend time praying about how they can begin to deepen these relationships. This could be as simple as inviting a new friend to eat lunch or grab some coffee, or maybe they can invite a neighbor or two over to watch a TV show or movie together.

The goal is to make sure these friends don't feel like a project. If your group member has never initiated a conversation with an acquaintance beyond "Hi, how are you?" suddenly asking him or her to come over for dinner each week will seem strange for both parties.

This may be a slow process. The goal is simply to get to know and develop a new friend. Of course, the hope is that the love of Jesus will shine through your group members' lives and that over time spiritual things will naturally come up in conversation.

IDEA 17

Reality TV

Sometimes it can be difficult to invite unchurched friends to a "Christian" event held at church. While the regular members of your group are comfortable in a church environment, their friends are being asked to overcome two hurdles: They don't know most of the people, and they aren't familiar with the setting of your church.

A more inviting setting can be a recurring event held at a home. A fun event could be watching a TV reality show together each week. Shows such as *American Idol* and *Survivor* have enjoyed loyal followings of people who feel strongly about who they'd like to see win. A show such as *Extreme Makeover: Home Edition* can also be fun, as each episode stands alone and there's an element of service and bettering a family's life. Fans of these shows are going to watch them anyway, so why not watch them together and make it a fun event?

If you choose a show in which a contestant is "voted off" each week, make that part of your fun. Each person who attends could be assigned to one of the contestants (either randomly or by choice). Whoever gets voted off that week has to bring the refreshments for the next week! If you have a large number of people, two people can represent each TV contestant.

Encourage each regular group member to invite to this event at least one friend who doesn't normally attend your group. The focus should be on friends who may not know Jesus personally yet or friends who are looking for a place to belong. A healthy mix of regulars and new people will help everyone feel more at ease.

While this event is focused on building new or solidifying existing friendships between young adults and their friends, you can easily start discussions with the following questions:

- Who would you choose to vote off, and why?
- Why do some people on this show seem to be well-liked and others don't?
- What types of people seem to do well on these shows?
- If you went on the show, do you think you'd do well? Why or why not?

These shouldn't be "official" discussions but could be topics to bring up during commercials or at the end of the show if it seems natural.

IDEA 18

Shark!

On a warm night during the summer, hold a fun event that will be easy to invite friends to—and will keep them cool as well.

The event is simply this: Watch the movie *Jaws* in a swimming pool! Locate a private swimming pool you can use for the evening. Check with people in your church.

You might want to begin after the dinner hour in order to avoid thinking about food. Or you can start earlier and then make a cookout part of the event. Regardless of the dinner decision, provide snacks and drinks for the movie.

As people arrive, they can spend time eating, swimming, and talking with each other. Since you'll need a sound system for the movie, have fun playing beach music. Tropical decorations might be fun, too. As soon as it gets dark enough, set up a portable movie screen and an LCD projector, and connect the sound system. If you don't have these, look into borrowing them from another church or renting them. Of course, you need electricity, so be sure to check that out ahead of time (and make sure the cord's nowhere near the pool!).

Then start the movie! Let people know in advance that they can bring water rafts if they want to float and watch the movie in the water. Some people may want to watch from the "sidelines," and if so, let them know that's OK, too.

At the end of the night, be sure to thank people for coming, remind them that they're welcome at your church and young adult group meetings, and invite them to your group's next event.

IDEA 19

Which Way to the Mall?

Providing transportation for a shopping trip can be a perfect way for those involved in your ministry to meet other young adults in your community. This idea works great if you live near a university or community college but can also be effective at apartment buildings or mobile-home communities.

Choose a time many people have shopping to do. This might be at the end of August when school is about to start or at the beginning of December when people are buying Christmas gifts. Choose a Saturday that will work for members of your group to go shopping. You'll need as many volunteer drivers as you can get.

Make signs to promote the event. Let people know that you'll be meeting at their dorm, apartment building, or community room to provide free rides to a local shopping center or discount store. Make sure you let them know what time you'll be meeting and how long you'll be gone. Include a line at the bottom of your signs that says something such as "A free service provided by the young adult ministry at [name of church]" so people will know who you are.

If the event is successful, consider making it a monthly thing. You might have repeat "customers," and they will spread the word to neighbors and friends. As you develop relationships with them, they may start asking questions about why you're doing this. What a perfect opportunity to invite them to visit your group, where they can learn more about a relationship with God!

IDEA 20

Well, Umm, Jesus Died, and Umm, You Know...

If young adults are trying to build relationships with others in order to eventually share the gospel, then it's important that they actually know how to clearly communicate the truth of the gospel to someone who has never heard it.

The first step is for them to be able to tell the story of how they came to have a personal relationship with Jesus Christ, without using churchy words or phrases that someone might not understand.

Prepare your own personal faith story to share with the group. Then guide group members through the process of telling their own stories.

A clear, easy-to-share account consists of three parts:

1. What your life looked like before you trusted Jesus.
2. A clear explanation of how you chose to put your faith in Jesus (so others can follow and learn from your example).
3. How your life has changed because of your relationship with Jesus.

For those who became Christians at an early age, the story might be a little different. They'll still want to share how they're growing in Christ and perhaps life changes that have occurred as they have continued following him.

Your story of your relationship with Jesus should last *three minutes* at most. You don't want to dominate conversations. Three minutes is more than enough time to cover the basics. Leave people asking questions and wanting to talk to you again, rather than wanting to avoid long conversations with you in the future!

After you've shared your own testimony with the group, hand out paper and pens, and give people five to 10 minutes to jot down notes about their own stories. These notes should center on the three points listed above. Participants should list highlights of what happened before and after they trusted Jesus and a clear explanation of how they chose to follow him.

Next, have them begin writing out the *exact words* they'd use to talk with another person, keeping in mind the three-minute target. This is important because this is often where the churchy words will creep in. The question people should ask themselves is "If the person I'm talking to has never set foot in a church, would he or she understand what I mean?"

Change any words that need further explanation. For example, instead of saying "saved" or "accepted Christ," say "decided to follow Christ" or "decided to become a Christian." Avoid words such as *justified, sanctified, blood of Jesus,* or any other theological words. The idea of a personal faith story is to share the story of how you decided to trust in Christ, not to explain all the mysteries of Christ's life, death, and resurrection!

Once group members have finished a rough draft, have them share their stories with people sitting near them. Pairs are best for the sake of time. They'll probably be reading from their notes, but they should focus on dialoguing with the people they're sharing with. The listeners should keep their ears open for churchy words or phrases. When the speaker has finished, have the listener share two or three good things about the person's presentation and one thing to work on. If the speaker went a lot longer than three minutes, help think through what could be cut out to make the account shorter. Then have people within the pairs switch roles.

Once everyone has shared, have the whole group talk about what they've learned. Encourage them to continue working on and perfecting their stories. The goal is not to put together a "perfect" story but one that's easy to share in conversation. If someone is stumbling over words, it might be difficult to share the story with a friend—and this is the most important story they can share!

Section Seven: Service

If outreach (discussed in Section Six) is about growing your group, then service is about reaching beyond your group. It's simply being the arms and legs, hands and feet of Jesus to the world. Serving means that you see the needs of people and meet them; in return, the people you serve catch a glimpse of Jesus.

You can also think of service as kind of a safe level of evangelism. While most of the time you'll simply be helping others, the Bible says, "Always be prepared to give an answer to everyone who asks you to give the reason for the hope that you have. But do this with gentleness and respect" (1 Peter 3:15). In other words, be ready if people ask what is motivating you to serve.

Who will young adults serve? Homeless men, abused women, at-risk kids, international students, lonely seniors, faithful church members, other young adults, and each other—the kinds of people your group can serve is almost endless.

Serving others has a hidden benefit that many people overlook. Sure, service projects help the people we serve. But service also does something to us. God doesn't mean for service to merely be a way to correct the wrongs of the world. He also wants to use service to shape our hearts into Christ-like character. Christian service can break our addictions to our own needs, shake us into awareness, and expose us to a kind of love of that we might not otherwise be aware of.

Following Jesus' Example

Read John 13:1-17 and the "to know" information in the following paragraph. Then, as a group, talk through the "to discuss" questions. Finally, help everyone remember the quick study by doing the activity in the "to do" section.

To know:

In Palestine, walking was the normal mode of travel. Because the streets weren't much more than dusty paths, dirty and sweaty feet were inevitable, and a good host provided foot washing for his guests upon their arrival. This unpleasant task was usually assigned to one of the lowest-ranking servants.

In John 13, the meal is being served, but the foot washing hasn't yet taken place. Apparently, the disciples in charge of setting up the dinner had failed to arrange for a servant to do it. Jesus was the last person the disciples expected to wash their feet. Peter's objection reveals his discomfort with this reversal of roles. But Jesus explains that he's demonstrating an attitude he wants his followers to imitate. Greatness is found in service to others.

We are to follow Jesus' example and serve others. But it's really not that great a sacrifice. John 13:17 tells us that if we willingly follow Jesus' command, we'll be blessed. We'll gain an inner peace and contentment that goes beyond external circumstances.

To discuss:

- What attitudes and actions did Jesus carry out that demonstrated his servanthood?
- What attitudes and actions do modern-day servants display?
- What are some ways we can serve others the way Jesus did?

• If we serve others in these ways, what kinds of responses can we expect from those around us?
• What do we allow to get in the way of following Jesus' example and command to serve others?

To do:

Use a towel to remind your group of Jesus' demonstration of service. Say, "This towel represents our special service award. When the towel comes to you, tell how you've seen another person in our group serve others in some way. Then give the towel to that person. Each person should receive the towel one time."

Begin by telling of someone's service and giving that person the towel. Try to choose someone who's not an obvious choice. When everyone has received the towel, lead the group in a closing prayer. Thank God for his example of a servant attitude and for his promise of blessing when we serve others.

4 Leader Tips on Service

TIP 1

3 Questions to Determine What Projects to Do

There are three essential questions you need to ask when serving others. How you answer can make or break the effectiveness of your service ministry. Let's take a look at the questions:

1. *What strategy will you use?* You'll quickly discover a lot of needy and valuable people and organizations within your community. Unfortunately, it's impossible to meet the needs of them all. Your group might choose to provide one-time help to many different local organizations to gain greater exposure, or you might decide to focus on one organization and place all your resources there.

2. *How will you implement your strategy?* In other words, who will serve, and how will you get them involved? One method is to have a young adult ministry Day of Service. Arrange for several outreach service opportunities for the same day. Or if your young adult ministry has small groups, each group can serve together. As the ministry leader, you provide options—potential organizations and projects that you check out in advance—and the individuals or groups choose the project they want to get plugged into.

3. *How frequently will you reach out?* It's easy both to overcommit and to under-commit when it comes to serving others. You want to challenge the young adults in your ministry to make service more than just an option, but you don't want to demand that they overcommit to doing projects every week. Suggest that people serve once a quarter, and provide opportunity to serve more frequently if they desire.

TIP 2

3 Ways to Equip Young Adults to Share Their Faith

Part of doing service projects is being ready to respond if someone wants to make a commitment to Christ. While this isn't the focus of your service ministries, you'll want to equip and train your group members with the how-tos of evangelism. Here are a few things to keep in mind:

1. If your young adult ministry or church doesn't already have tools to use for training, look for tools that work well in your ministry setting. Start with *Becoming a Contagious Christian* by Bill Hybels and *The Church of Irresistible Influence* by Robert Lewis.

2. Provide the opportunity for members of your group to go through evangelism training at strategic times for a few weeks to a few months before your service activity. This will allow them to get practical information on how to start a spiritual conversation, how to share their own faith stories, how to talk through questions they might encounter, how to pray with someone who wants to receive Christ, and how to follow up and disciple someone.

3. Realize that you can't train everyone. But God can still use untrained and unequipped participants from your group to accomplish his purposes. Don't get discouraged if a smaller number of young adults comes to your training classes than you'd hoped for.

TIP 3

Service Survey

Use the questionnaire on page 203 to learn about the talents and interests of the young adults in your group. Distribute and collect the surveys once a year, and be sure to have new group members complete surveys as well.

TIP 4

Media Releases

Sending a press release to local media outlets is a great way to publicize the service your group is doing. See the sample on page 204. Keep these things in mind when submitting a release to the media.

- Newspapers often need to receive material several days or weeks in advance. Find out when your newspaper's deadline is, and send in your press release early. TV and radio stations might use something more last-minute.
- Don't be wordy, and don't use churchy language. Include only the pertinent information about your event.
- Be sure to include your name, address, phone number, and e-mail address in case someone at the media outlet needs to contact you to clarify the details or get more information.

"I Can Help" Questionnaire

Here are some ways you can help the young adult ministry at our church. Please check all the ways you'd be willing to pitch in.

Don't worry! Checking a box doesn't mean you're committed! We just need to know what kind of resources we have right here in our own group to help us better plan our activities. We'll contact you about each service opportunity, and you'll have a chance then to say yes or no.

___ Lead a Bible study
___ Be a mentor
___ Be a "mentee"
___ Write or design publicity pieces
___ Do general office work
___ Serve meals
___ Plan and prepare meals
___ Bring treats
___ Speak at an event
___ Facilitate a small-group discussion
___ Be on a planning committee
___ Shop for supplies
___ Organize supplies
___ Organize volunteers
___ Provide transportation
___ Contact new members by phone
___ Visit new members
___ Be on a welcoming team
___ Sing or play special music
___ Lead group singing
___ Work at a registration table
___ Host an event in your home
___ Take photos
___ Other: ______________________
___ Other: ______________________
___ Other: ______________________

Name: ______________________

Address: ______________________

____

____

Phone number: ______________________

____

E-mail address: ______________________

____

____

Sample Media Release

For Immediate Release

Date: ______________________________

Church: ______________________________

____

Contact person: ______________________________

____

Phone number/e-mail address: ______________________________

____

Event: ______________________________

____

____

Date of event: ______________________________

____

The young adult group from First Church will be collecting items for Community Food Bank on Saturday, October 20, from 1 p.m. to 4 p.m. at First and Main. The public is encouraged to bring non-perishable food items or cash donations to the drop-off site.

First Church is located at 5213 North Wyndham Road, Chelsea Springs. The young adult group—for college students, recent college graduates, singles, and others from 18-30—meets at the church each Sunday at 9 a.m. and at Cuppa Joe Coffee (6778 Briarhurst Blvd) on Wednesdays at 7 p.m. For more information, call 557-555-4265.

30 Service Ideas

IDEA 1
Conversational Partners

Nearly 600,000 students from other lands are presently studying in the United States, many of them from countries closed to Christianity. They've come here to get a degree, but while they're here, they also want to experience American culture. Often they're also interested in understanding what Christianity is all about. Unfortunately, most of them will make few American friends, and only a tiny percentage will ever see the inside of an American home.

Nearly every college and university with any enrollment of international students has some sort of "conversational English" program for their students from non-English-speaking countries. Members of your group can share in a cross-cultural adventure, make new friends, and promote faith in God in other lands without ever leaving home. Call your local college's international student services office and offer your services. They will caution you about proselytizing students, which you can assure them you are not about. The goal is to befriend and to serve.

Most international students actually have a fairly good grasp of English, as generally they have to pass language proficiency tests to enroll in schools here. However, they're often insecure about their spoken English and deeply desire to talk more like Americans. Conversational partners get together at an agreed-upon time just to talk. The Americans gently help with pronunciation and vocabulary, but the basic format is simply to talk about your respective lives and countries.

If several members of your group do this, you can celebrate the end of each semester by bringing all the conversational partners together for a picnic or cookout.

IDEA 2
Wal-Mart Runs

When students from other countries enroll in classes in the United States, they don't just experience separation from family and friends. Often, international students have no idea where or how to shop in the United States. Your group can provide a wonderful service to new friends from other countries by offering transportation and guidance regarding shopping on a weekly or monthly basis.

Check with the international student services office of a local college or university to help you determine a good time and place to originate your shopping runs. You'll need to borrow a church van, and early each semester you may also need a pickup truck or a trailer to help these students do the heavy shopping they need to furnish their living spaces.

Though quite familiar to virtually all Americans, stores such as Wal-Mart or Target can appear completely threatening to students who are used to buying products from street stands. One member of your group for every three or four international students is a good ratio to help people find what they need, to help them pay for their purchases, and to get everything transported.

IDEA 3
Tutoring At-Risk Kids

Large numbers of children in America grow up with little support or encouragement from adults of any sort. Tragic at all ages, especially in middle and high school, the lack of appropriate role models and mentors has many educational, social, and spiritual consequences. But this is a need the young adults in your group can do something about.

Communicate with the guidance counselor of a middle school or high school near your church. Offer to provide free tutoring services, assuring the counselor that this isn't a smokescreen for proselytizing. Let the counselor guide you on how to make your services available to the students. Recruit young adults with education in a variety of subjects, and set a time shortly after school is out for them to be available at your church facility.

If your building has a family life center, gym, or other less-threatening area, use that for the tutoring center. Have light, inexpensive, and healthy snacks available. Don't overwhelm those who venture in with too much attention.

You'll spend time helping kids with math and history, but you'll also hear heartbreaking stories about family situations and precarious circumstances. Your numbers will fluctuate wildly, and some students you come to care about may just stop coming. But keep in mind that you are planting seeds of truth and watering lives with love.

Be sure to check with your church office about providing background checks for anyone who works with teenagers, and find out if church policy is adequate for the school whose students you're helping as well. If not, a very useful resource is Group's Church Volunteer Central network (churchvolunteercentral.com), a subscriber-based site that not only contains ready-made background checks and parental consent forms but also many articles; online training resources; and many other useful tools to help recruit, equip, retain, and lead church volunteers.

Follow the standards without grumbling or exception, making sure there's no opportunity for negative situations to develop.

IDEA 4
A Night Out or a Makeover In

In most cities the average citizen tends to be somewhat aware of homeless men wandering the streets, eating at soup kitchens, and sleeping in shelters. But in most communities, there are also lesser-known shelters for women who have had to flee their homes—often due to abuse and often with their children.

Women's shelters tend to be large and overcrowded facilities occupied by hurting women in transition who are trying to figure out their next steps. Often they've left home with little more than the clothes on their backs. While the women in these shelters often form close bonds with each other, sometimes residents can feel closed in.

Contact the director of a shelter in your community, and ask how you might be of service. In order for the women in the shelter to go out (for shopping, bowling, dinner, or whatever you choose to treat them to), another part of your group will need to entertain their children at the shelter. Find out the shelter's standards about child care and background checks, and follow them explicitly. Make sure the kids have a great time, too, with special foods and activities.

Members of your group could also spend an evening with the women in the shelter providing facials, manicures, and hairstyling. In the world of uncertainty in which these women dwell, such pampering is a welcome diversion and encouragement. Again, provide something fun for the kids while the moms are being pampered.

IDEA 5

Power Ties and Savvy Suits

What does it take to break the cycle of poverty and homelessness? Education and vocational training are two critical components of helping people get jobs and get back on their feet. But there's another important need that's often overlooked: professional appearance.

It may seem trite to suggest that clothing is important, but the reality is that it's essential to look nice and feel confident during job interviews. When someone facing financial hardship has only outdated thrift-store slacks, a stained dress shirt, and a tie that doesn't match, he's likely to feel self-conscious and belittled. Sadly, this person's unprofessional appearance is likely to be noticed by the potential employer and may prevent him from receiving the job. And in many cases, this lack of appropriate attire may prevent the person from showing up at an interview at all.

Mobilize your group to meet this real need in a very practical way by coordinating a "business clothes" drive within your congregation. Collect new or used-but-nice dress shirts, suits, ties, men's and women's dress shoes, business skirts, and women's business jackets.

When your group has collected a good amount of clothing, donate the items to an organization that helps people transition out of unemployment, such as a homeless shelter, a shelter for abused women, a men's home, or a rehabilitation program for former prison inmates or drug addicts.

IDEA 6

Grocery Express

In the old days, elderly folks could call up their favorite grocery stores, dictate a list of groceries, and have them delivered to their front doors. Such days are long gone, unless the older individuals happen to be Internet-savvy or have relatives nearby. As mobility declines, simply obtaining food for the week becomes more and more of a challenge.

There might be people within your own church or community who can use help with grocery shopping. Some people may just need transportation to get to the market and back. Others may feel overwhelmed by the whole situation and may desire someone else to do their shopping for them. Either way, your group can help.

Patience and flexibility are the major attributes you will need as you assist these folks who generally feel that food prices are out of control and that nothing is quite as good as it used to be. But you'll learn a lot and build good friendships with some fine people. If you actually do the purchasing for the elderly people, ask them to be as specific as possible about what they want, and be sure to be as frugal as you can be in fulfilling those desires. Make sure your elderly friends get full receipts and exact change back!

This is a good Saturday morning activity for multiple members of your group. Meet for breakfast, pray together, and then head out to shop—or do the shopping first and meet up for lunch with the other members of your group.

IDEA 7

Adopt-an-Apartment

In many cities, homeless shelters are purchasing older motel or apartment buildings and complexes and creating "transitional housing" to assist the homeless in getting back on their feet. Generally these buildings are "distressed" when acquired, and the homeless ministries have to completely rehab them.

Why not encourage your group to adopt an apartment? The young adults in your group can provide funding and labor to create a warm place to live.

Contact the homeless shelter, and find out who is in charge of facilities. Then take some young adults to walk through the building to catch a vision for what a difference they can make. Claim an apartment as your group's, and figure out the best plan for remodeling. Perhaps you could do a weekend blitz and get the apartment ready to go or at least get a good start on the project and get a number of your group members enthused about the project. This is a great opportunity for various group members to use their unique gifts and skills to contribute to the whole.

In most cases such transitional housing is offered furnished, so another part of the project is actually making the place livable. Young adults love doing "total makeovers," creating a place they themselves would enjoy living in. When you've finished, bring back everyone who had a hand in the rehabilitation process, and hold a dedication service for the apartment.

IDEA 8
Back-to-School Kits

One of the rites of passage for young adults is the first stirring of nostalgia, especially about elementary school days. Even if they didn't like school, few didn't enjoy the annual rush of buying all new school supplies and feeling ready to go. Your group can provide that feeling for children who might not otherwise ever experience it.

Most school districts hand out lists of what children of each grade should have when they go back to school. Your group can get one of those lists and pool resources to purchase the needed items. It's OK to be a little extravagant if your group wants to provide kids with items *they* always desired but never owned in their own school days.

Pack all the purchases in an age-appropriate book bag, label it with the grade level of the contents, and pass it on to an agency that distributes supplies.

IDEA 9
Adult Day-Care Activities

Families that care for elderly family members in their own homes often have to seek supplemental care during the day when the caregivers are at work. So adult day-care centers have flourished in recent years, catering to the needs of these families. Often these centers care for widely divergent groups of elderly and disabled adults, providing health care and offering activities for their clients. But often they are understaffed and can't possibly provide the level of personal contact that many people desire.

Your young adult ministry could take on a particular time each week to visit with and provide activities for the clients at a local adult day-care facility. After discussing options with the professional staff, your group could create a rotating schedule of entertaining activities. Talent shows, bingo and other games, and singalongs are all popular options. This is one setting where the staff will allow or might even encourage Christian music and teaching.

IDEA 10
Kids' Ministry Production Crew

Children these days grow up in a high-tech world. They tend to have access to all sorts of media and computer technologies from early ages. They're surrounded by top-quality graphics and productions in all areas of life—except maybe church. The average children's minister desires to put together professional-grade audio/video materials for children's programs but seldom has the time or the staff to do it.

Today's young adults have unprecedented access to tech tools and media resources and often have a great deal of experience in working with both. A team of young adults offering even a few hours a week to assist the children's ministry will provide a huge service to the staff.

Recruit a team of willing workers, and then set up an initial meeting with children's ministry leaders, offering assistance for one event. If that works well, the relationship will expand naturally from there.

IDEA 11
"Will Work for Food" Pantry

Today's young adults are often caught between two competing impulses—giving to those who ask, yet being suspicious about people who make their needs known. This is especially true with individuals who stand by the side of the road with "will work for food" signs. Young adults usually have no way of hiring anyone and may not feel it's appropriate to just give money.

One solution is a "will work for food" pantry at an accessible location where group members can store up single-serving-size foods. Group members can load up bags of nutrition and take them out to "the street." Some might even want to keep a bag or two of collected food in their cars.

To provide for someone on the side of the road, the food can't require a can opener, cooking, or utensils. Single-serving tuna fish snack kits, pop-top pudding packs that don't require refrigeration, peanut butter crackers, bottled water, and granola bars are all ideal foods for such a pantry.

IDEA 12

A Night With the Homeless

One of the most amazing and controversial things Jesus did was spend time with the poor and the untouchables of his time. He taught them and healed them, yes, but he also ate with them, spent time in their homes, and listened to them (Luke 5:27-32).

Offer your group the challenge of spending the night in a homeless shelter, in order to experience some of what it is like to be homeless and to meet some of the people Jesus has asked us to serve. Contact local shelters and halfway homes—preferably ones your church already has a relationship with—and ask for permission for some of your young adults to spend the night with the residents. Explain that the goal is for these young people to better understand the struggles and indignities that homeless people face in order to be better equipped to serve them.

Then broach the subject with your young adult group. Read some Scripture passages (Matthew 25:31-46; Luke 14:12-14; 16:19-26; James 2:1-6) as inspiration. Not everyone will be comfortable with this, so don't push anyone into it. Select a date, and get firm commitments. Assign groups of no fewer than two and no more than three to each shelter or halfway home. Meet with participants at least once before the experience to talk about what it will be like. Offer reading about poverty, such as *Why the Homeless Don't Have Homes and What to Do About It* by Micheal Elliott. Many members of your group will be anxious about what to say if other residents ask what they are doing there. Tell them to be honest and say they are there to listen and learn. Most of the residents will respect this and welcome the opportunity to share their experiences.

Drop off the groups at the shelters before the evening meal if one is provided, and pick them up in the morning when the shelters let out. Plan for some time afterward to discuss their experiences. Encourage some of the young adults who participate to share their experiences with your entire group or with the entire church.

IDEA 13
Senior Beauty Shop

Most young adults enjoy plenty of human contact. But many elderly people receive less and less of healing and loving human touch as they age.

Jesus showed how powerful touch could be. He put his hands on people in order to heal them—people who others would never touch for fear of becoming unclean. Those who reached out to touch him were miraculously healed, even if they were just able to touch his cloak (Matthew 14:36; Mark 5:25-34).

Offer some healing touch to elderly people with a manicure ministry. Call a local nursing home or retirement home, and ask if you can set up a time for your young adult group to visit and give simple manicures to residents. Have your volunteers bring hand lotion, tissues, nail files, nail polish, and nail polish remover, and set up a miniature beauty salon.

Don't have volunteers cut cuticles or do anything that would present a potential hygiene risk. They can just rub lotion on the hands, massage the hands and arms up to the elbows, smooth the ends of the nails, wipe the lotion off the nails with a tissue, and apply polish. (This service will probably appeal to women, but encourage elderly men to receive this service, too, if they wish. Just skip the nail polish or apply clear polish.)

Another great idea is to have your volunteers visit elderly or shut-in members of your congregation and provide them with manicures in their homes. While they are ministering to the hands of the elderly, your volunteers can fulfill another of their needs by just listening and conversing.

IDEA 14
Janitor's Day Off

Church janitors work very long hours, often logging a lot of evening and weekend overtime. Their work is hard and often goes unrecognized. Organize a group of young adult volunteers to give your janitor or janitors a much-deserved day off one week or weekend day.

Talk to the person who supervises the janitor(s) at your church, and ask what day would be easiest for your crew to take over. Get a list of daily janitorial duties, and note where all the supplies are kept. Then have volunteers sign up for one- to two-hour shifts, enough to make up a full eight-hour day. Assign duties from the list to each shift. Some will need to be repeated each shift, such as emptying the trash cans and checking the bathrooms for toilet paper and paper towels.

While you might want to surprise the janitor about his or her day off, give advance notice so he or she can plan activities for the day and make notes for your volunteer janitors.

IDEA 15
Little Brothers and Sisters

Set up a mentoring program for members of your group to guide children in your congregation. For inspiration, read Matthew 18:1-5; 19:13-14 and Mark 9:36-37 to your group. Ask each volunteer to commit to at least a year of mentoring. Emphasize that this will be a significant commitment of time, a commitment to a relationship that could potentially last for a lifetime. Their task will be to meet with "little brothers and sisters" once a month or more to talk about what they're learning in Sunday school, do homework, play sports, or engage in other activities.

It is also important to remember that it is wise—and in some places legally necessary—to pre-screen volunteers who are watching children as part of a church-sanctioned activity. Your church may already have a screening or background check system in place. If not, Group's Church Volunteer Central network is a very useful resource (see Idea 3 for more details).

Once your volunteer system is in place, put a notice in your church's bulletin that parents of children ages 8-13 can sign their children up for a Big Christian Brother or Sister. Talk to interested parents about what kind of role the big brother or big sister will play in their children's lives, and have them complete forms about their children with information about the children's performance in school and their interests outside of school. Depending on the number of children who sign up, you might want to prioritize children of single parents or narrow the age span of eligible children.

Then match men to little brothers and women to little sisters. Plan a fun Sunday afternoon event to announce the matches. Celebrate with some games (such as Three-Legged Race, Tug of War, or a water-balloon toss) as the pairs get to know one another.

You might have to rematch if people move away or simply can't sustain their commitment. Periodically check in with both the parents and volunteers to make sure the relationships are progressing well.

IDEA 16

Adopt a Grandparent

Organize a group to visit a retirement home in your community. Often such facilities already have a system for using volunteer help.

Gather your group beforehand to encourage them to think about the experience people have when they move into an assisted living facility. Elderly people go through a range of different experiences and emotions when they reach a point in their lives when they need ongoing medical and life care. Sometimes they feel as if their independence has been taken away—a challenge to anyone's self-esteem. Sometimes they feel abandoned or alone, particularly if their families live elsewhere. Yet they often have interesting stories to tell. Volunteers at such care facilities will usually find very receptive guests.

Discuss God's concern with those who are in need or ignored. Read Exodus 22:21-23. Discuss why we are called to take care of those who have nothing material to offer us in return. Throughout the Old Testament, God held the Israelites accountable for the way they treated widows, orphans, and foreigners living within their territory. Prophets such as Amos chastised the Jewish people whenever they neglected those among them who couldn't defend themselves. God wants us to pay attention to those who are ignored by a society of wealth and advancement.

When you visit the retirement home, you might be asked to lead a Bingo game, visit people who cannot leave their beds, or play music. Ask the facility how you can be of most use; chances are, they'll be ready with an answer.

IDEA 17
Orphans and Widows

James 1:27 defines religion that is "pure and faultless" as "look[ing] after orphans and widows in their distress." In the early church, these people needed to be protected, as they were outside the protective boundaries of a family unit. In our society, elderly people often lack family nearby to help care for them and their needs. As a young adult group, adopt an elderly individual (or couple). The person could be a member of your church or someone who lives near the church. Try to choose someone who is unable to get around very well, who needs some help and companionship. Look for someone who doesn't have a lot of family in the area.

Throughout the year, provide services for your adopted senior, such as mowing the grass, raking leaves, or shoveling snow. There may be other services you can provide inside the house, such as moving furniture or doing any cleaning the senior is unable to do alone. You can also plant flowers, bake cookies, or prepare a meal. Some members of your group could volunteer to be on call either to take your adopted senior to the store, doctor, or church or to run errands.

Don't get so wrapped up in chores, however, that you forget the aspect of companionship. Encourage your volunteers to take time out from raking to strike up a conversation with your adopted senior. Make sure to send birthday and holiday cards and stop by for periodic visits.

If your young adult group is large, adopt more than one senior.

IDEA 18

Building on Rock

Gather a group to spend a day with Habitat for Humanity. Habitat builds houses all over the world with the express purpose of eliminating substandard housing. Look up Habitat in your local phone book, or find your nearest chapter online (www.habitat.org). Ask when and where their current builds are happening.

Members of your group can take part in building a nice house at all stages of the labor. The project is overseen by contractors, carpenters, plumbers, and other building professionals.

Gather the volunteers from your group to begin the workday with prayer and reflection. Read Matthew 7:24-27; 1 Corinthians 3:7-15; and Ephesians 2:19-22. Remember that the purpose of participating in this project is to offer a model of Christ's love through your actions. The gifts we give to others, even something as big as a house, will one day pass away. But the gift of love and life offered in Jesus is eternal.

IDEA 19

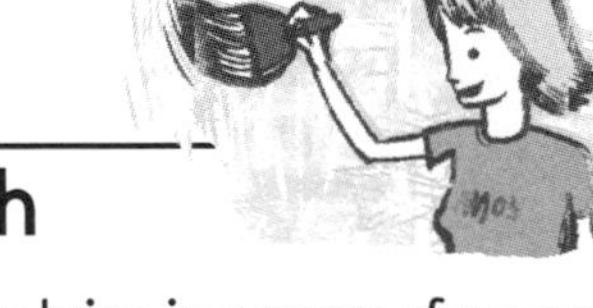

Serving the Big "C" Church

Organize a service day for a neighboring church. Offer to bring in a group of young adults to do whatever the church needs: cleaning bathrooms, yardwork, stuffing envelopes. Take care of cleaning supplies so the church has no expenses.

Church leaders can sometimes be sensitive that another church is in competition with them. Assure the church you're serving that you don't want any publicity announcing to their congregation what you've done; you just want to offer the service as a gift and be a good neighbor.

Afterward, debrief your group's volunteers with a time of reflection. Read 1 Corinthians 12. Reflect on what it means to be a part of the same body with other churches that are part of the same church with you.

IDEA 20

Maid to Order

Service can extend all the way...to another member of your group. Organize a maid exchange within the young adult group. Once a month, put together a team to clean and polish the home of another member of the group. Standardize the service: bathrooms, windows, vacuuming, dishes, dusting, garbage, maybe even laundry!

Afterward, order pizza, and have a time of discussion about what it means to serve one another. Read John 13:3-17. Discuss the model that Jesus set with his willingness to do even the most menial tasks for his friends.

IDEA 21

Undercover Pastoral Care

Organize a day of mission and espionage! When your church's pastor is at work, do some undercover service projects. Wash the car in the parking lot, and deliver home-baked cookies anonymously to the front office of the church. Make plans with the pastor's spouse or family to mow the lawn.

Discuss how people who serve also need to be served. While we're sometimes tempted to turn service outward toward groups of needy people, 1 Timothy 5:17 reminds us also that those "who direct the affairs of the church well are worthy of double honor, especially those whose work is preaching and teaching."

Similarly, take your secret ministry on the road. Find out what nonprofit organizations in town provide service to the community with severely limited staff. Perhaps the staff of a homeless shelter provides food for the needy. How often are they thanked for their work? Take them out to dinner as a thanks for the many dinners they've served.

IDEA 22

A Day in the Park

Invite young adults to spend a Saturday morning in a local park for a service project. Contact the local parks department to determine a park that would benefit from litter cleanup. Come equipped with garbage bags, latex gloves, environment-friendly disinfectant, Bibles, and a picnic brunch.

When your volunteers arrive, invite them to read aloud Scriptures about God's awesome creation (Genesis 1:1-2:3; Psalm 8; and Romans 1:20). Then get busy caring for God's created world.

Assign jobs to teams such as litter pickup, sanitation of kids' playground equipment, removal of debris, or trail maintenance.

When the work is done, gather back together to debrief from the experience. Talk about simple ways to care for God's creation on a daily basis, or discuss other means of serving the neighborhood through practical cleanup projects. Spend time in prayer, praising God for the beautiful world he has made and committing to live as good stewards of his creation.

Wrap things up with a picnic brunch—and be sure to clean up after yourselves!

IDEA 23
Mission-Minded Mail

Mobilize young adults to spend an evening supporting foreign missionaries by assembling care packages.

Contact missionaries supported by your church to learn about any specific items they'd like to receive from home. Make a list of their requests, plus any other ideas you have, such as Christian magazines, nonperishable food products difficult to find overseas (such as bubble gum or peanut butter), kids' art supplies, personal hygiene products, pictures, books, greeting cards, or computer disks.

Invite young adults to sign up for items they'll donate to the care packages. Set a date and time for a "care-package party," giving participants a month or so to buy the supplies. Add fun to the party by making it an international potluck. Ask all participants to bring a food item from another part of the world to share with the group.

After you eat, get down to business. First, profile the missionaries the group will be mailing packages to. Pass around pictures of the missionary families, tell participants about the specific work these missionaries are doing, and give background information about the part of the world where the missionaries live. The book *Operation World* by Patrick Johnstone is a great resource that provides detailed information about the spiritual climate in various countries around the world. You can also find helpful information on the Web at www.joshuaproject.net.

Form teams to fill shoe boxes with the items your group collected. Add personal notes of encouragement and favorite Bible verses. When the care packages are assembled, spend time as a group praying for the intended recipients. Ask God to encourage them, protect them, and empower them for ministry.

Don't forget to mail your care packages!

IDEA 24
Petty Cash for Practical Needs

Begin the tradition of taking a monthly benevolence-fund offering in your young adult group. Explain that the money they give in this offering will be kept specifically for ministry to those in the community or church family who are in financial need.

Each time your Group takes a benevolence offering, invite someone to read aloud Isaiah 58:6-8. Then lead the group in prayer, asking God to make clear the specific ways he wants you to spend the money to meet the needs of others. Ask group members to prayerfully keep their ears and eyes open for practical needs that the group's benevolence fund might be able to address. These might include

- buying a crib for a friend in a crisis pregnancy
- paying a car-repair bill for an unemployed neighbor
- helping a struggling college student buy books for class
- making a financial donation to a ministry for the homeless
- giving a grocery-store gift certificate to a family on welfare

Encourage the whole group to be involved in deciding how and when to spend the money, to maintain a sense of ownership over the ministry. Whenever possible, do the giving anonymously. Also, be sure group members keep the discussion of people's needs in confidence.

IDEA 25

Behind-the-Scenes Sunday

Many churches have an annual "youth Sunday" when teenagers take over the church service and perform various functions such as ushering, reading Scripture, leading music, and even preaching. Revamp this concept by telling your pastor you want to have a covert "young adults Sunday" where members of your group take over all the behind-the-scenes work of the church.

The key phrase here is "behind-the-scenes"! No spotlight involved. Instead, serve your greater church family by giving a much-needed break to the volunteers who work tirelessly each Sunday to make church happen. Enlist group members to do jobs such as running the soundboard and PowerPoint, serving as greeters and ushers, creating and photocopying bulletins, caring for infants in the nursery, prepping the Sunday school supplies, providing coffee in the foyer, and cleaning up after the church service. Of course, don't forget the most important job of all: praying that God would use the service to speak to his people and to touch the hearts of visitors who attend.

Keep in mind that your church may require background checks and references for volunteers who work with children. Be sure members of your group comply with these requirements, and plan ahead so all paperwork and background checks can be performed as necessary.

After the special behind-the-scenes service is done, thank young adults for their efforts. Encourage them to consider ways they can continue to serve the church family on a regular basis through volunteering in some of these behind-the-scenes jobs.

IDEA 26

Free Couples' Night

Organize a day-care night on a Saturday evening. Be sure to round up plenty of young adult volunteers to staff every age group from babies to middle schoolers.

Volunteers will need to be screened ahead of time, following your church's policy for background checks on anyone who'll have contact with children.

Use the church newsletter and bulletin to announce the event to young families in your church. Encourage them to use the time as a date night. You can even extend the invitation to young families in the community. Just be careful—if it's too well publicized, you may be overwhelmed!

Discuss your intentions with a local day-care provider and your church's nursery directors. Carefully note their suggestions on how to make the event fun and safe. Specifically, you'll want to set up a process for parents to check their children in and out, taking every appropriate safety precaution. To avoid any hint of impropriety, have volunteers work in teams so no adult is ever left alone with a child. Again, if your church does not already have a screening or background check system in place, Group's Church Volunteer Central site is a very useful resource for these materials (see Idea 3 in this section for more details).

Have a certified first-responder on hand to provide emergency care. Make sure participating families leave phone numbers where they can be reached in case of emergency. Set a firm pickup deadline for parents.

Provide snacks, movies, and recreation time in your church's gym or fellowship hall. Set up tables covered with craft paper and crayons for younger kids, and create a game area with cards, board games, and video games for older children. Be sure to recruit a cleanup crew to help repair the damages when the children have headed home!

IDEA 27

Help Line

Challenge your group to buy a cell-phone plan that can be used as a 24-hour help hotline. Because the phone will be used only to receive calls, look for a plan with unlimited "call-me" minutes.

Ask volunteers who are interested in answering calls to meet in advance to share insights on various problems young adults have and how they can offer encouragement in times of distress.

Anticipate all the possible scenarios that affect young adults—unplanned pregnancy, debt, depression, school or career related stress. If possible, ask a certified crisis counselor to attend your volunteer training sessions to offer suggestions about how to listen and help.

Pass around a sign-up sheet, and ask volunteers to sign up for a 24-hour period, if possible. Responsibilities include answering the hotline during their designated time slot and offering encouragement to the caller. For their safety, instruct your volunteers to disclose no personal information in the course of the call but do their best to offer calming words of comfort and Scripture to people who are hurting.

Advertise the hotline with newspaper and radio ads and fliers posted on bulletin boards in stores, in restaurants, and on college campuses. Make it clear that the hotline is staffed by volunteers, not professionals, who are there to listen and encourage, not to offer advice.

Provide volunteers with a list of community services and references for more serious calls they might get. Your help line is a place where someone will listen; emergency situations can be referred to professionals who are prepared to offer advice and assistance.

IDEA 28

Car Questions?

If individuals in your group are blessed with car-genius, put them to work on a Saturday morning. Invite people in your church and/or your greater community to an appointment with a "car doctor." Advertise the event in the paper and on the radio, and put up fliers around town.

The goal isn't to fix the cars but to help diagnose problems and suggest a course of action. Car doctors can refer people to reliable and trustworthy mechanics and give them a sense of confidence as they enter a somewhat intimidating realm.

To get more people in your group involved—even those of you who know nothing about cars—combine the event with free car washes. Even if cars still need repairs to run great, they'll drive away *looking* great!

IDEA 29

Tournament Time

Many recent college graduates become depressed when their once-active college lifestyle is replaced by sedentary office work. Ask your group to plan, host, and clean up after a volleyball or basketball tournament for young adults in the community.

Recruit a team to plan the event, schedule a gym (a church gym is ideal), and line up referees. These officials can be hired through a local parks and recreation department. Or if you're on a tight budget, ask some die-hard sports lovers in your church to brush up on game rules and ref the tournament for free. Provide the usual drinks and snacks.

An advertising committee can brainstorm ways to get the word out. Advertise in the newspaper and on radio stations. Create fliers to be distributed at libraries, coffee shops, and bookstores—wherever young adults hang out.

For a nice touch, create awards for all your participants, to be presented at the end of the tournament.

IDEA 30

Ambush Lawn Service

Organize yard crews to ride in pickups or vans with mowers, rakes, lawn trimmers—anything they might need to manicure a yard. Look through your church directory for names and addresses of people in the church who might not have the time or capabilities to keep up on yardwork, and send in the ambush yard team to the rescue! Call the individuals before you arrive to ask permission to clean up their yards.

Your ambush team could also plant shrubs and flowers to make things really beautiful. Be sure to ask the yard owners if they want these plantings, as some regular care will be involved after the ambush team is long gone. If the owners go for it, ask local nurseries for donations of materials or if they offer discounts to nonprofit/community groups.

Send your crew out in teams of three or four, and have them meet back for homemade ice cream when all their hard work is done!